Who's Number One?

Who's Number One?

Joe White

Tyndale House Publishers, Inc.
Wheaton, Illinois

Scripture quotations, unless otherwise noted, are from the *New American Standard Bible,* © 1960, 1962, 1963, 1971, 1972, 1973 by the Lockman Foundation. Quotations marked NIV are from *The Holy Bible, New International Version,* © 1978 by New York International Bible Society. Quotations marked TLB are from *The Living Bible,* © 1971 by Tyndale House Publishers. Quotations marked KJV are from the King James Version of the Bible.

First printing, October 1986

Library of Congress Catalog Card Number 86-50464
ISBN 0-8423-8215-1
Copyright © 1986 by Joe White
Printed in the United States of America

*To Mom and Dad,
the most "I'm-third" people
in the world*

CONTENTS

1

Who's Number One?

She ran up and down the stadium side-lines Saturday after Saturday, wearing her red-and-blue SMU cheerleading outfit and cheering on her beloved team. She stayed as close to the football as the chalky white sidelines would allow. She gave eleven tired, sweaty players everything a cheerleader possibly could. I first noticed this exuberant brown-eyed girl as I was pulled from the game for missing yet another tackle.

"Get in there, Joe! Come on! We've got to win!" I don't know if it was at Georgia or Michigan or Texas, but I'll never forget the girl who poured her heart out for the SMU team.

Not only did our peppy, acrobatic cheerleader perform well on the football field, she also marched to the beat of a different drummer. Debbie Jo was different. She studied hard at night while her roommates partied. She drank Cokes at fraternity parties while the other girls got wasted. She was so pure on her dates that our outside linebacker dropped her after three dates, claiming she "wasn't fun enough."

Three years later I was the lucky one who married this most unusual girl. Debbie Jo taught me a lot about the drive it takes to be a winner. She also taught me how to put God first in day-to-day living. I wasn't the only one attracted to her, of course. Debbie Jo's Christian character earned her many dedicated friends on campus. She knew how to love people and how to put their needs above her own. And she was great fun to be with.

Playing against Ohio State one Saturday, I heard a chant that I'd never heard before. Our football team and cheerleaders stood in amazement as thousands of spectators screamed in unison, "We're Number One! We're Number One!" The chant spread like wildfire across America. Soon, almost everyone made the claim.

Banners billboarded the slogan to the television audience; cheerleaders screamed it to their stadium crowds; receivers danced around the end zone, flashing the Number One sign proudly overhead. Interestingly enough, not only did everyone claim to be Number One but almost everyone acted like it, too, both on and off the field.

The 1970s were the beginning of the now rampant teenage and college-age problems of heavy drugs, heavy drinking, pregnancies and abortions, and suicide. I grew to realize that living like you were Number One almost guaranteed your days would be filled with problems that seemed larger than life itself.

Every day the mailman delivers to our rural mailbox

a stack of letters from teenagers and college students who are pleading for a helping hand as their lives as Number One have brought them problems they can't handle alone anymore. Here are a few candid sentences that reflect the same condition. They'll probably sound familiar to you because the same problems have infiltrated every junior high, high school, and university in America.

This year has really been difficult for me. At the beginning of the year I really felt strong about not drinking and having sex. As the year went on, I guess it just got easier and easier to slip. I know I did some things I shouldn't have, but I think I've really learned from my mistakes. I know there is no such thing as a big or small sin, but I know God made me see the light before I let any big major sins ruin my life (or reputation). He's been so good to me! And I know if I just keep my morals set, and keep my eyes on God, everything will work out perfect.

Football was the big sport at my senior high school, and if you were good and became a starter, then you became very popular. Well, I became popular and this was something I was not used to, and it went right to my head. Well, popular people partied and I wanted to be the B.M.O.C., so this boy partied hearty and soon paid for it. I look back now and see what kind of witness I could have been on the team and in school. Oh, what a waste!

I'm fourteen and I am in a little trouble. It all began about four years ago, when I started to drift away from God. Directly after this, I began to experiment with all the things that I had never done when I was going to church. To say the least, I got in a little bit of trouble. You see, this year I'm a freshman in high school, and I really like this one guy. But a guy I used to hang around with keeps on harassing both him and myself. I "looked for love in all the wrong places," and my ex-boyfriend won't let me forget that. I'm really confused. I've tried suicide many times, and have had some of my best friends just totally destroy themselves by using drugs, and I don't want to have anything to do with any of them anymore, but they won't leave me alone. I

*don't feel right anymore, and I really need to find God again. I
really need your help right now. I'm afraid if I don't get help,
something might happen.*

You can see what results when a person really begins to believe he himself is Number One. You can also
see, if you are a Christian, that Someone Else is Number One, Someone bigger than us. Long before the
first college cheerleader beamed upward into a packed
football stadium and encouraged that now familiar
chant, "We're Number One! We're Number One!" a
loving voice from no one less than our very Creator
said, "I'm Number One. I was Number One. I am
Number One. And I'll always be Number One."

It is interesting to me (and, frankly, heartbreaking
at times) that the further removed we—the people he
created in his finest craftsmanship—get from the living truth of his stance, the more disastrous our lives
become both as individuals and as a whole population.

Evidence for the mess we've made is all around
us—on TV, for instance. Now, I admit I don't watch
much television. Rolling around the living room with
my children in a family wrestling match or laughing
through a Monopoly game with little tykes who don't
know the difference between a one-dollar bill and
Boardwalk is a lot more exciting and uplifting than a
wasted hour in front of the boob tube. But recently I
slipped. While traveling across Oklahoma, I spent the
night at a Holiday Inn; while there I checked out the
programming on a cable-connected nineteen-inch set.
After fifteen minutes of scanning the channels I was
bewildered. First, there was a movie (I believe it won
an Oscar) that cursed God and the name Jesus Christ

repeatedly. I was offended just like I would be if some-one cursed my best friend. I switched through a cou-ple of music video channels and watched people wor-ship rock stars who jeered at God and claimed the way to find satisfaction in life is through violence, rebel-lion, and perverted sex. Channel after channel dis-played the philosophy of the late twentieth century: "I'm Number One. My friends are Number Two. My music and TV are Number Three and God . . . well, he's somewhere near the end of the list." His calming voice assures me that this is all wrong.

In the beginning was the Word, and the Word was with God, and the Word was God. He [Jesus Christ] was in the beginning with God (John 1:1).

I am the Lord your God, . . . You shall have no other gods before Me (Exodus 20:3).

Jesus Christ is the same yesterday and today, yes, and forever (Hebrews 13:8).

The Bible, the greatest love letter ever written, has one message that is repeated over and over and under-lined with Christ's life and blood:

Love me first.
Love others second.
And love yourself third. If you remember this order, I'll make your life happy, rewarding, and fulfilling.

As Jesus approached the last historical week of his thirty-three year stay on earth, he was confronted in the synagogue by the leading interpreters of the Jew-ish law.

As they sought to trap him with various theological

questions, he always gave answers that astounded their minds with accurate simplicity. They said, "Sir, what is the one great commandment? Sum it all up in one sentence. How can we truly know God's will for our lives?" In his typically straightforward and authoritative manner Jesus replied, "'You shall love the Lord your God with all your heart, and with all your soul, and with all your mind.' This is the greatest and foremost commandment. And the second is like it, 'You shall love your neighbor as yourself.' On these two commandments depends the whole Law and the Prophets" (Matthew 22:33-40).

In other words, God is first, others are second, and you are third.

This one great commandment has come to you straight from God. To misunderstand it means drastic consequences—now and for eternity.

As I write I will seek to put my heart, mind, and soul into the pages of this book to help you know the joy, the satisfaction, and the love that God has placed in my life since I asked him to sit in the "driver's seat" of my life fifteen terrific years ago.

FOR REFLECTION

1. What is the primary thing that each of the letters in this chapter have in common?

2. What are some indications that a person isn't putting God first in every area?

3. Can you memorize Matthew 22:37? Try it.

4. What is the three-letter name that is repeated again and again in this chapter?

5. How is it the key to understanding the great theme of this chapter?

6. What is the four-letter word that is repeated?

7. What does that valuable word mean to you as Jesus uses it here?

2

Making God Number One

I have always been intrigued by the miracle that happens every time a lowly caterpillar turns into a beautiful butterfly.

Our scientists label the process *metamorphosis,* but, short of the divine workmanship of God, they don't really know how to explain it. It stands out as a unique happening in time. (God has loaded this earth with tiny miracles if we'll open our eyes to his splendor.)

I used to watch caterpillars crawling around in the dirt, helplessly struggling for survival. Each one seems so unaware of anything except its own drive for survival. Then that hairy little worm enfolds itself into a mummy, and it goes to sleep for a long time.

In a matter of weeks the soft little package begins to open. A totally transformed body, mind, and purpose emerges in the likeness of a dazzling butterfly that soars above the earth. The transformation is a living illustration of how a really radical change can occur. God is in charge. He can change a life. He can take what you give him and make it beautiful!

A friend told me about a seventeen-year-old girl who had been destroyed by a twenty-four-year-old guy who had told her he loved her and soon took advantage of her sexually, leaving behind a broken heart and a broken life.

I immediately called Sue on the phone and asked her if she'd mind us talking. Reluctantly, she agreed to come over. As we sat down to talk I could see the hurt. Her eyes were dead. She had gained twenty-plus pounds in her lack of care for herself. She had abandoned a promising athletic career in gymnastics. She really didn't care about living. She was merely existing.

For an hour or two I talked, I listened, I dried her tears, I dried my tears. As the afternoon turned into early evening, however, she began to accept God's great "I'll-never-give-up-on-you" love. When she read slowly through Revelation 3:20 and recognized that great statement of Jesus to be a personal invitation from God to her, she bowed her head in prayer. As big tears of relief streamed from her eyes, she asked Jesus Christ to come into her heart, to forgive her sins, and to be her personal Lord and Savior. She had been as low as the lowly caterpillar, but a butterfly flew away. Later on the following letter was waiting in the mailbox for me:

Dear Joe,

Thank you for helping me bring Christ into my life. Running into you at this time in my life when I have been kind of emotionally lost was the realization that Christ and God really are there for me to turn to. Opening the door and letting him into my life is the most wonderful feeling I've ever had. I am truly saved. I am so anxious to learn and strengthen my faith.

I have already started reading the Bible you gave me and I have a feeling that church this Sunday will be different than it's ever been. For the first time I feel like I have the Christian faith.

With love always,
Sue

Another letter from a seventeen-year-old friend underlines Sue's discovery:

Dear Joe,

I want to tell you how great it is to be a Christian—a real Christian! Now I'm finding so much strength! I can't describe it. Joe, I was always skeptical of how true the Christ story was, happening so long ago, and I knew there was a Christ and all, but now I know he's real. I know he's alive and I know he's with me, and the happiness is indescribable. I thought if I was a Christian I would be a prude and wishy-washy and bored, but it's exactly the opposite! It makes me feel good about me! It's just bubbling excitement of happiness within me right now as I write! It's really hard, but I'm trying to put him in complete control of my life.

Love in him,
Maria

CHRIST'S INVITATION,
THE GREATEST INVITATION OF ALL TIME

"Here I am!"	*Listen, I've got something great to tell you!*
"I stand at the door"	*The door to your heart*
"and knock"	*Jesus is a gentleman. He doesn't barge into your life.*
"If anyone"	*Yes, that means you.*
"hears my voice"	*You might be hearing it right now.*

"and opens the door"	*The handle is on the inside—for you to open.*
"I will come in"	*Not "maybe"—not "I might"—I will!*
"and eat with him, and he with me" Revelation 3:20 (NIV)	*Forever—I'll fellowship with you forever. I'll make you a butterfly.*

The disco bar in Paris, France, was crowded. The room was dark and lit for mood. A fire broke out near the front door and swept the building. The party people rushed frantically for the exits. Curtains had been installed to cover the exit signs and doors; consequently, they were hard to find. Those who found the doors grabbed the handles and shoved with all their might. The doors didn't budge, for they had been nailed shut to keep intruders out. Everyone in the disco perished in the fire because of the nails in the doors.

Your mind and your heart have many rooms. In each room you house a very important area of your life. In one you have your friends, in another your entertainment, in others your schoolwork, your parents, your daily quiet time, etc. Jesus longs (he "knocks") to be in every room to fill it with his purity and his love.

The handle to each room is on the inside. You have to open it and let him in. As you willfully sin and keep him out, you put a curtain over the door. It becomes hard to find. Soon you don't even care when you sin. You become numb to your sinful ways. "It doesn't affect me," you say. "I can handle it on my own." Jesus knocks again. You put nails in the door to keep him out. Then the tragedy comes. Someone dies. You get sick. Your boyfriend leaves you. Your girlfriend says she doesn't love you anymore. You rush frantically to the door and scream, "God, help me!"

Today is the day to let him in. Get your hammer out and pull out those nails! Don't wait for the fire! Don't wait till it's too late!

Eighty-five percent of the people who wait until after their eighteenth birthday to ask Jesus in never ask him.

Ninety percent of those who wait until they are twenty-one perish without him.

Don't be one of the millions who plead in a crisis, "Why did I wait so long?"

If you've never asked God in to change you into a butterfly, you may want to do it now. The "I'm Third" life begins with a personal relationship between you and Jesus Christ.

FOR REFLECTION

1. What did Jesus mean in John 3 when he told Nicodemus, "You must be born again"?

2. Who can a just and holy God allow into heaven?

3. When did you become a "butterfly"? How did it happen?

4. What does it take to make someone a true Christian?

5. Why is doing good things not enough to save us? Why is going to church not enough? Why is growing up in a Christian family not enough?

6. When your little boy or little girl (someday) asks you if he or she will get to heaven, what will you tell him?

3

Try God?

A bumper sticker was plastered on the back of a new car that zoomed past me on a busy Interstate somewhere near Dallas, Texas. It simply said, "Try God." I've thought about that slogan a lot, and I strongly believe that this "try it on" mentality is causing more misunderstanding, more false hopes, more broken dreams, than any concept of God that man has ever invented.

Try this dress on.
Try this new recipe.
Try this new football offense.
Try this grip on your golf club.
But don't try God!

A young American sailor stood bewildered on the deck of an American ship at daybreak on December 7, 1941, as the sky became instantly filled with Japanese aircraft. "Tora! Tora! Tora!" The shock he experienced as two-thirds of the U.S. fleet was crippled in Pearl

Harbor spread like an earthquake across the islands. In the midst of the blitz, a Japanese Zero crash-landed into the ship deck. The plane did not explode upon impact. The American sailor rushed to the Zero and yanked the cockpit off the dismembered plane. To his amazement his eyes were met squarely by the trembling, almost petrified, gaze of a fifteen-year-old Japanese boy who had been instructed to fly this plane on its one-way trip from Japan to Pearl Harbor. The Japanese kamikaze was locked and chained to the seat! When he left home that Sunday morning he left on a one-way mission that he knew would end in death on the deck of an American ship. That's how committed he was to the Japanese emperor's cause. He wasn't "dabbling." He wasn't "trying" the Japanese military life. He was committed.

You don't try God! When Jesus gave his all-time great invitation, "If you believe then you shall live," he meant that if you'll lock and chain your life in the cockpit of his love, if you'll stake your life on his love for you, then you'll know God. Then you'll know happiness. Then you'll know inner peace that won't need a cheap sex thrill or chemical high or security based on looks, clothes, money, and popularity, etc. "I will fill you up," Jesus said, "when you give your life to me."

Christianity is the total commitment
of the total person
for the total life
and
Christianity is giving God all that you have
in exchange for God giving you all that he has.

CONFORMED OR TRANSFORMED?

I urge you therefore, brethren, by the mercies of God, to present your bodies a living and holy sacrifice, acceptable to God, which is your spiritual service of worship. And do not be conformed to this world, but be transformed by the renewing of your mind, that you may prove what the will of God is, that which is good and acceptable and perfect (Romans 12:1, 2).

When you place a thermometer in a new room it quickly adjusts itself to the temperature of that air. It changes when the atmosphere changes. When you place a thermostat in the same environment it eventually changes the atmosphere to the temperature it prescribes.

A "Thermometer Christian" tries God. But when someone comes around with something more fun, he goes back to his old way of life and leaves God behind. When the urge to lust or backbite a friend or get bitter over a hurt or disobey his parents comes, he changes. That is the tragedy of peer pressure. The "friends" change the Christian girl or guy to something he no longer believes in.

A "Thermostat Christian" on the other hand, determines in his heart to follow Christ. He locks himself to Jesus' standard of living. Jesus becomes the only "peer pressure." Either the atmosphere changes or the Christian gets a new atmosphere. He doesn't change. He doesn't look back to his old life-style. He sets the pace at home, at school, at parties, on dates, everywhere.

My four children were fascinated when (on a youth group trip to Cancun, Mexico) I caught a chameleon for them. This little six-inch lizard captivated my kids because of the mechanism that enables it to change colors as it changes environment. When it jumped upon a leaf, it turned a camouflaging light green. When it jumped upon a branch, it corresponded with a quick transition to dark brown. Four pairs of little eyes were fixed on this amazing creature that could look just like whatever he chose for a perch!

If there's one characteristic that is sure to bring a Christian problems as he goes through his student years, it is the chameleon mentality. "I am who I'm with. You wear Polo, I wear Polo. You smoke, I smoke. You go to church, I go to church. You pray, I pray. You talk trash, I talk trash."

Jesus went through the crucifixion to wipe out your past and say, "Now stand up for what you believe. Dare to be different. Commit your life to me and I will lift you up into a brand new creation that your friends will look at in awe. And they'll be affected by this dedicated life you lead."

I have been crucified with Christ; and it is no longer I who live, but Christ lives in me; and the life which I now live in the flesh I live by faith in the Son of God, who loved me, and delivered Himself up for me (Galatians 2:20).

FOR REFLECTION

1. *Read Revelation 3:15, 16. What does it say to you?*

2. *What is a lukewarm person?*

3. *How do you live "hot" for God?*

4. Why does lukewarm Christianity cause a person so many problems?

5. What is your desire for your life today in regard to this chapter?

4

He Did
What for Me?

$\mathcal{A}$ team of six full-time camp directors and I are privileged to travel each winter for two months in an effort to recruit our summer staff of some 750 Christian athletes. Our recruiting team is composed of ex-college athletes, who enjoy each other's friendship to the maximum.

As we travel we love to hear each other's old sports stories. One member of our team is a six-foot-six basketball player who recently finished an exciting career at the University of Arkansas. On our last trip together I talked to Brad extensively about his most memorable game with the powerful Russian national team. With a gleam in his eyes Brad recalled the details of the clash that was settled in an overtime in Little Rock, Arkansas. One of Brad's most surprising memories was the way the Russians were awed at our players' blue jeans. As the teams would encounter each other before and after the game, the Russians would stare at our jeans and even reach out to touch the fabric that every

American has a closet full of. Imagine not being able to buy blue jeans!

A trip to Mexico or almost any foreign country will reveal dozens of other striking reminders of luxuries enjoyed in America by the rich and poor alike, things that we seldom take time to truly appreciate. On a trip to Tijuana, Mexico, two decades ago I saw thousands of people living in tiny houses made of old cardboard boxes, throwaway pieces of plywood, and wooden crates. We have so much and often don't even acknowledge our abundance of blessings!

The gift we most universally take for granted is the greatest gift that any man or woman ever had in his possession. And this gift is available to anyone, no matter what financial status you occupy or what nation you live in. It is the gift of salvation.

Let me illustrate the significance of this great gift with a story from our country's pioneer days. Lisa was a fourteen-year-old girl traveling across the plains of Kansas with her family and a dozen or more other families in the mid-1850s. The trip took months to complete behind the slow-moving oxen of the wagon train.

The tiny band of pioneers climbed up and over a medium-sized plateau in the rolling, dry, brushland of northern Kansas. As the wagons hit level ground after the climb, the pioneers saw a raging brush fire coming hard and fast toward them, powered by a strong west wind.

The fire raged as far to the north and to the south as their eyes could see. They panicked as they realized there was no way around it. Soon the wagon train would be overtaken and consumed in the flames.

In the midst of the confusion, Lisa's father had an idea. He lit a torch and began to set fires behind the wagon train. Other men got the idea and set a whole wall of fire on the east side of the wagons. The same wind that blew the fire toward them blew the new fire away from them, leaving behind the burned-out bare ground. Lisa's father issued a command, "Bring the wagons to the rear three hundred feet." As the wagons rolled onto the freshly charred ground, the fire in the west got dangerously close. The travelers could now feel the heat. Lisa screamed, "The fire is catching up with us! We're going to die!" Lisa's dad caught her firmly around the shoulders with his loving arms. "No, Lisa, it will not catch us. For we're now standing where the fire has already been."

And so are we. The place where "the fire has already been" is on the cross, where Jesus suffered so we wouldn't have to. When we stand beneath the cross and put our trust in the Jesus who died there, we are safe from the fire. The fires of hell are still raging and many choose to stand in Satan's destructive pathway. But thanks be to God, when any person turns from his sin and gives his life to Christ, he is "standing where the fire has already been" and will watch Satan's fire go out right before his eyes.

Growing up in a Christian family, I heard about the cross before I could scarcely walk or talk. Each Sunday brought back the story with growing familiarity. It became so familiar that in the eighth or ninth grade I didn't really care anymore. I had heard about it so much that it had little meaning for me. But later on I began to appreciate more completely what had been given personally to me in the pinnacle of history, Jesus' crucifixion and resurrection.

I didn't really appreciate the cross until I realized that as Jesus went through those trials he was spit upon disgustingly. To me, that spit represents all the filthiest thoughts and actions that you or I have allowed in our lives through poor choice of TV, movies, magazines, music, etc. I didn't really appreciate the cross until I realized the slugs in the face and the beating with sticks that Jesus voluntarily endured represent all of the anger and hatred and bitterness that my life and your life have known.

I don't think I truly appreciated the cross until I understood that the torturous flogging that was laid on his back was necessary to heal you and me in our sin-sick, rebellious moments against God. I did not appreciate Jesus Christ until I understood that he wore a crown of thorns so that you and I might have the privilege of wearing the Crown of Eternal Life when we pass through the portals of death.

The cross was just another piece of wood to me until I understood that God had to turn his face away from his precious Son. Yes, for the only time in all eternity God and Jesus were separated and by his sovereign will God would not reach down and rescue his Son from our sinful madness.

I know what that separation is like. One winter day I came home from three weeks of travel and suffered through a twenty-four-hour bout with the flu. I was sick. It was the kind of flu that takes everything out of you. It is also highly contagious.

As I stumbled through our front door and headed for the bedroom, my youngest boy, Cooper, came running across the floor. "Daddy! I want to hold you!" I passed him by, ducked into the bedroom, shut the door, and fell into bed.

Cooper didn't understand. ("I haven't seen my Daddy in three weeks and I want a hug. Did he forget me?" I'm sure thoughts of rejection were racing through his mind.) He began to cry as he pounded softly on my door. "Let me in, Daddy. I want to hold you. Let me in!" For three to five minutes he sobbed in his hurt. I cried in my helplessness. I was too sick to go to him. I loved him too much to give him my disease. Our separation broke my heart.

For the first time in my life I caught a glimpse of what God must have felt as he had to turn his face from his Son and briefly abandon him because of our sickness (sin) that Jesus became for you and me. I am sure that the pain of being separated from the Father far surpassed any physical pain that Jesus had to suffer on that fateful day in history. But the painful separation was the great display of divine love, as the Apostle Paul realized: "But God demonstrates his love for us in this: While we were still sinners, Christ died for us" Romans 5:8, NIV).

What *kept* Jesus on the cross that day? Those nails? A tree shaped like a cross? The Roman guard? No. LOVE kept Jesus on the cross. LOVE—his love for you and me. I'm convinced that even if you'd been the only person on earth, he'd have done it all just for you.

Like a sacrificial lamb, Jesus Christ took on the sins

of every man who dared to trust him with his life. He saw the face of you, me, and every man and woman of all time whose sins he bore. And yet, in spite of the maximum price he paid, he could see many faces saying, "So what! Big deal! I don't care. I want to do my own thing. I don't want to give up the fun I'm having for Jesus! Maybe later!" And he knew the day would come when he'd have to turn his face and reject even you or me or anyone who had rejected him—the greatest mistake that anyone could ever make.

So many people avoid that mistake. They respond freely to the gift of divine forgiveness and love. Some of these people are well-known in the entertainment field.

I had a most enjoyable talk recently with Philip Bailey, one of the most talented male vocalists in recording history. Formerly with Earth, Wind, and Fire, and now doing his own contemporary Christian thing, Philip Bailey has sold almost fifty million albums and won seven Grammies. The first question I asked him was, "Philip, if you could sing one song to all the young people in America, what would it be?" After having pressed fifty million records, his reply was astounding, "I'd sing, 'Jesus loves me, this I know, for the Bible tells me so.'"

FOR REFLECTION

1. Why did Jesus have to die? Couldn't God have thought of an easier way?

2. What would life be like if there was no forgiveness?

3. *After all that Jesus went through, what do you think he expects of us now?*

4. *What was the hardest part of the crucifixion for him? Why?*

5. *How much would you say God loves you?*

5

A Change of Clothes

$\mathcal{S}$he's "sweet sixteen." As she walks hurriedly from her new car to her first-hour algebra class
she's hoping that her brand new clothes will catch the
eye of that special guy whose locker is two doors down
the hall. Her arms clutch tightly a three-hole spiral
notebook (with very few completed math problems)
and her textbook that hasn't made sense to her since
the x^2y^2 was first explained six weeks ago. Perhaps the
now dog-eared issue of *Seventeen* that's partially hid-
den inside her notebook cover tells the familiar story.
Styles, makeup, and new clothes are a lot more exciting to this sixteen-year-old than algebra will ever be.

She could be thirteen—or a twenty-one-year-old
coed dashing out of the Kappa House at Ohio State—
and the story would be pretty much the same. New
clothes are always "what's happening" from New York
to L.A. and every stop in between. With guys it isn't
much different. A new pair of Wranglers or Nike
warm-ups feel mighty fine. The styles and brands may

vary but the fact remains—it is great to take off those tired old rags and get into something new.

Styles change, jeans fade, shirts lose buttons, and it all costs a ton of money—but there's one set of new clothes that never gets old!

I've seen a lot of style shows—both officially tailored and fleeting across campus—but nothing is as impressive as that change of "clothing" that happens to a guy or girl whose life becomes sincerely committed to Jesus Christ. As God's Spirit fills (controls and empowers) the heart, the internal result is more beautiful than the most stunning page of *Glamour, Seventeen, Sports Illustrated,* or *Teen.*

Sometimes the change of "clothing" happens at times of desperation. I'll never forget the angry, hurt, and turned-off frown that looked permanently tattooed on Melinda's face as she stalked cautiously into our youth group that certain Sunday night. Her dad was an alcoholic who had chosen suicide over life. What he left behind was a confused seventeen-year-old high school junior who was well on her way to a similar fate. For four straight weeks she hugged the back wall of our often-crowded meeting room. She refused to join in the craziness that typified our hilarious skits and rowdy music. When talk time came, however, she soaked in every word. She didn't miss a meeting. Two more weeks went by and I got the phone call I'd been waiting for. It was Melinda. She wanted to talk. After an hour of the most straightforward and honest one-to-one question-and-answer times I've ever spent, Melinda bowed her head humbly and asked Jesus Christ to come into her life. It was more than the words of a prayer. She gave her heart to him.

What took place in that girl's life in the next four months is hard to describe. I can only say it was beautiful to watch.

No caterpillar who crawled in the dirt before has ever come close to capturing the breathtaking transition that took place in Melinda's life as she burst into a life as fantastically beautiful as that of a butterfly.

Those brown eyes began to twinkle. The wrinkles which had grown out of a miserable outlook on life were superseded by a pair of dimples and a smile that was deeply meaningful and attractive.

Melinda had a new set of clothes. She wore them every day. Our youth group came alive as more and more of her friends came around to see about this man Jesus who had changed the heart of their friend so drastically.

I've seen Melinda's story happen hundreds of times on high school and college campuses across the nation.

A big, strong, fast NFL football player called me from a pro athletes' conference. "I've gotta talk to you." His voice sounded urgent. I planned to be in his home state within two weeks, so we made a two-hour appointment and got together.

He was a Christian, but he wasn't satisfied with his walk with the Lord. What was he playing football for? How should he handle his fame and money? Why was he struggling with things in his life like looking at scantily dressed girls in magazines and carrying lustful thoughts in his mind?

We got out pen and paper and began to write. I asked, "What is really important to you in life? What are the things that need to change in your life? Where do those impure thoughts begin? Why did God allow you to play in the NFL?" Questions like these led him to set some very special goals for his life.

I directed him to decide what to "put off"—eliminate from his life.

- He decided to "put off" any and all magazines that had girls dressed less than completely.
- He decided to "put off" all X, R, and most PG movies, plus any TV that had bad language and suggestive scenes.
- He decided to "put off" selfishness and greed with his money.
- He decided to "put off" procrastinating on the truly important things in his life, like having a daily quiet time, and having strong moral convictions.

Next I asked him to decide what he needed to "put on"—to begin to do in his life.

- He decided to commit himself to a minimum of twenty minutes a day studying God's Word.
- He decided to "put on" at least five minutes a day praying to God.
- He decided to "put on" a commitment to pure entertainment that would provide pure thoughts.
- He decided to "put on" Scripture memorizing with a minimum of two verses per week.

A month later I saw him again. He had a giant grin across his face. I could tell he really felt good about something! He sat me down and opened a well-organized notebook that had a daily journal of his progress. The journal stated each of his goals clearly. It had a summary of each day's Bible study. It had a list of daily prayer requests. He had successfully "put off" his negative areas and "put on" a new life-style that he felt good about.

Alice came to me about a long-standing problem with a guy she continued to lust for. We had a "put off" and "put on" talk. She was ready to change.

Helen wanted to do something about her growing dependence on alcohol, which was leading to problems at home, at school, and on dates. An open heart and an honest list of "put off" and "put on" is helping her greatly now. She is beginning to follow Paul's advice to the Colossians:

Therefore consider the members of your earthly body as dead to immorality, impurity, passion, evil desire, and greed, which amounts to idolatry. . . . Put them all aside: anger, wrath, malice, slander, and abusive speech from your mouth. . . .

And so, as those who have been chosen of God, holy and beloved, put on a heart of compassion, kindness, humility, gentleness and patience; . . . And beyond all these things put on love, which is the perfect bond of unity (Colossians 3:5, 8, 12, 14).

If you ever feel the need to "put off" some "rags" of your life, I suggest you do the following. You'll be amazed how it works.

1. Thank God for all he's done for you. Sometimes you may not feel like it, but mention everything you can think of.

2. Get out a pencil and paper and draw a line down the middle (top to bottom). On the top of the left column write in big letters "Put Off." On the top line of the right column write "Put On." Now list all the things (be specific) under "Put Off" that you need to

change—places you go, things you do, attitudes you have that don't bring out the best in you. Keep in mind your parents, your friends, your dates, your study habits, your parties, your daily quiet time, your eating habits, etc. Under the "Put On" column, list the things you need to begin to do. Again be very specific, and don't allow any cop-outs like "I'll try" (trying doesn't do anything). Write "I will."

At the bottom of the page write the word "When" with a long blank beside it. Fill in the blank with the day and time you plan to begin this new life with "new clothes" on. If you really want the best in your life, do it again and again throughout your life.

FOR REFLECTION

1. *What is a problem you need to come to grips with?*

2. *What are the things you need to put off? Put on?*

3. *Why is it so easy to put on new clothes and yet so difficult to change your personal habits?*

4. *If you could pick one character quality you'd like to have more of, what would it be?*

5. *How can you put that quality into your life more abundantly?*

6

A Continual Conversation

By Dave Maddox

I've met a lot of people who know how to communicate with students, but Dave Maddox is at the top of my list. Dave wrote this all-important chapter on talking to God. It is a trophy that you will thoroughly enjoy:

". . . this mystery, . . . which is Christ in you."

If what the Apostle Paul wrote in Colossians 1:27 is true, then every Christian is a miraculous mystery. The great mystery is that Jesus indwells the life of every believer. God desires to share life with each one of us in an individual and intimate way. Life becomes transformed once we grasp this amazing fact and continually act upon God's presence within us.

What difference does it make in your life that God is present with you? When you are alone, do you find that you spontaneously talk with your heavenly Father? When you attempt to pray, does your mind ponder his presence or wander from it? Do you find your prayers in a group to be geared more to that group or to God himself? How intimate is your conversation with him? Do you speak to him constantly?

These questions may leave you feeling inadequate or guilty. There was a point in my life in which I became painfully aware of how little I acted upon and responded to the presence of God. This awareness resulted from an experience in which I found myself more affected by the presence of a high school sophomore than by Almighty God.

Let me explain. During my days in seminary I did all my own repairs on my 1969 GTO. It was quite a racing machine. It had a four-hundred-cubic-inch engine, a four-barreled carburetor, four-speed transmission, and got four miles to the gallon. Unfortunately, I burned the clutch out of it and had to replace that part. The difficulty with clutch replacement is that one must remove the transmission to get to the clutch. I was successful in taking out the transmission and replacing the new clutch, but had difficulty when it came to getting the transmission to slide back into place. It just would not cooperate. No matter how hard I strained and groaned, it refused to slide back into place.

As I struggled with this frustrating project, a high school sophomore dropped by to see me. Mike had recently become a Christian and wanted to talk more about his new faith. We talked for a good while, and then I convinced him how much fun it would be to help me struggle with the heavy transmission. It seemed to be a good time also for Mike to witness the practical aspects of prayer, so I told him of the difficulty and explained our need to talk with the Lord about it.

"Lord," I said, "this transmission is giving me fits. Please help us get it back into place." God apparently refused. The transmission would not fit. Our further attempts were unsuccessful and we abandoned our efforts.

In this instance I was a model Christian. I asked God for help, accepted defeat, and never lost my temper. No doubt Mike was impressed with my faith.

The next afternoon I tried again. This time Mike was in school. I was alone under the GTO fighting with the one-hundred-pound transmission on my chest. I tried desperately to get it into place.

"Lord, again I ask for your help. Please make it go in like it is supposed to!" Again God refused. At this point my prayers changed in strategy—from request to demands. Then from demands to unbecoming verbage.

In response, God "opened the windows of heaven." It began pouring down rain. Of all places in the parking lot, I had picked the lowest area to work on the car. Soon I found myself lying in three inches of muddy water, ready to drown in frustration.

What a Dr. Jekyll and Mr. Hyde! A model Christian one day and behaving like an absolute pagan the next! What amazed me the most about it was that I was more concerned with my behavior around a high school sophomore than my behavior around God himself!

I acted appropriately in the presence of Mike, but did not act appropriately in the presence of the Almighty. But I am convinced that we can continually act on God's presence, and as we do so we will find a true transformation taking place. Paul teaches us that at every turn life links us to the Lord (Romans 14:8). We need only act on the presence of Christ in us from one moment to the next.

I have found that acting on the presence of God brings about a closeness with him. There are many important acts we perform to open ourselves to God, but this one practice seems to be perhaps the most deeply personal. Of course we need to be spending regular times in prayer, studying the Scriptures, writing our thoughts and requests out to God, even committing portions of the Scripture to memory and meditating upon those. These are vital in our walk with the Lord. Yet we need also to continually converse with him, to act upon his presence, to share our thoughts with him as readily as we would think them to ourselves.

Brother Lawrence was an amazing man who lived in the seventeenth century. He worked in a French religious community, serving mainly in a hospital kitchen. Neither a priest nor a monk, Brother Lawrence spent his time cooking and washing dishes. But he went about it in a unique way because of his awareness of the presence of God. He contributed to us an amazing discovery which has been called the "practice of the presence of God." His life became characteristic of a continual conversation with Christ. He writes: "I have found that we can establish ourselves in a sense of the presence of God by continually talking with him."[1] At first he found that to continually share his thoughts with God took discipline and effort, but in time the sharing became as natural to him as breathing.

He tells us: "You need to accustom yourself to continual conversation with him—a conversation that is free and simple. We need to recognize that God is intimately present with us and address him at every moment."[2]

A continual conversation! Is it even feasible? Paul teaches us to "delight" ourselves in the Lord and to find joy in him at all times (Philippians 4:4). This is the enjoyment of intimacy that God offers us. How infrequently we take advantage of what God offers.

I have suffered from a lack of spontaneous communication with God. One result is shallowness. Another is lack of intimacy. But God offers us more than we can imagine. I trust you too desire to move away from superficial Christianity and experience the richness in life that God has in store for you.

Perhaps no other verse encourages us to continually communicate with God more than 1 Thessalonians 5:17: "Pray without ceasing." I had always considered this verse to be a hyperbole, an exaggeration intended to make a point. Paul was exaggerating purely for the sake of emphasis. It seemed like something that should be said in a sermon, but not taken literally.

But we *do* need to converse continually with God, and, what's more, we *can*. Paul experienced this, and so did Brother Lawrence, fifteen hundred years later. We, too, can continually converse with God!

OBJECTIONS?

No doubt you are having some thoughts of objection. You may think it is unrealistic for normal people to be in constant communication with God. "This just isn't possible. Maybe Jesus could live this way, but he was the Son of God. Or maybe Paul, because he was the super-Christian of the first century. And maybe Brother Lawrence could pull it off because he worked in a religious hospital. What else did he have to think about!"

Before ruling continual prayer out as being unrealistic, consider this question: Are you satisfied with your relationship with God? If your answer is no, consider the possibility that your relationship could be deepened by continual communication

Frank Laubach was a man who made this great discovery. Laubach, who lived in the first half of this century and spent his life as a missionary to the Philippines, experienced a kind of spiritual dryness.

He wrote: "Two years ago a profound dissatisfaction led me to begin trying to line up my actions with the will of God about every fifteen minutes or every half hour. Other people to whom I confessed this intention said it was impossible. . . . You will object to this intense introspection. Do not try it unless you feel dissatisfied with your own relationship with the Lord."[3]

Like Brother Lawrence, Frank Laubach found it to be most difficult in the beginning. But as he continually gave himself to conversing with God, it became more and more natural. He claimed that under no circumstance would he ever go back to the dryness of his earlier days in which he only prayed at specified times.

The joy I myself have derived from my most feeble attempts to communicate with God continually are exhilarating. Of course it seems unrealistic at first, but God supplies the power for us to grow. He simply calls us to point ourselves in his direction. An effort to continually give our thoughts to him is only a matter of making our minds and wills available to him. God is the one who enables the communication to take place. We simply need to position ourselves to hear him.

You might also object by saying that continual conversation with God is unproductive. How can we always be talking to God and get anything done in this world?

Actually, unceasing prayer will *not* keep us from concentrating on our work. It enables us to share our work with him. When we relate to the Lord continually, the task at hand becomes his as well as ours. If you are mowing the grass, walking to school, working at a job, or engaged in a conversation, be continually mindful of him. Then your work becomes his as well, your walk becomes a time of conversation with him, and your dealings with others become divinely affected. There is no longer a distinction between the sacred and the secular, the spiritual and the unspiritual. God is involved in all your life because you are practicing his presence.

You might come up with another objection to resist Paul's instruction to "pray without ceasing." You might say that it is unhealthy. "Anyone who talks to God all the time is crazy! You've got to be a real person in the real world."

But what makes more sense—to continually talk to God, or to continually talk with yourself? According to modern psychology, we are always involved in a dialogue with ourselves—not just a monologue, but an actual dialogue. We will make a comment (not always aloud, of course) to ourselves, then answer back.

That dialogue seems to determine your self-image, your attitudes, your actions. If you are only talking to yourself, you get no other input, no counsel from an external source. And that is dangerous. People do terribly destructive things as a result of their self-dialogue. They rationalize crime and cruelty, harming others and themselves. Even suicide can result from self-dialogue. The victim convinces himself that this truly is the best option, and there's no outside voice to protest the decision.

Frank Laubach writes: "Instead of talking to yourself, form the habit of talking to Christ. Some of us who have done this find it so much better that we never want the other way again. No practice we have ever found has held the mind as much as this: making all thought a conversation with the Lord."[4]

HOW DO WE DO IT?

Let me share my own attempts to experience a continual conversation with God. Please understand that all of us need to continue having special "quiet times" with God, times of study and memorization of Scripture, and times of prayer, individually and with others. Yet I desire to go beyond these and communicate with the Lord at all times. I want to know what Paul meant when he said, "Pray without ceasing." I trust you do as well.

Let me encourage you by an admission that I am quite a beginner in seeking to have a continual conversation with God. I believe I am growing and moving toward more intimacy with the Lord. Where you are in comparison with others is not important; it is important that you are moving, growing.

Jesus said, "You are to be perfect, as your heavenly Father is perfect" (Matthew 5:48). Does that sound unrealistic? Of course! But understand that perfection has more to do with movement than the achievement of a goal. The word we translate as *perfection* is the Greek word *teleios*. The root of that word—*tel*—is a word from which we derive our words like *telegraph* and *telephone*. The concept has to do with "moving along a line." That is a picture of perfection—moving along a line toward a goal. Jesus Christ is both the line and the goal. Where you are on the line is not as important as the fact that you are on it and moving.

Even if you are moving only a tiny bit in unceasing prayer, you are doing well. Just get moving! I cannot compare myself with Brother Lawrence or Frank Laubach, yet I can be excited about progressing in intimacy with God.

For the sake of practicality, I will share my method of seeking to discover the joy of a continual conversation with God. It is quite simple, yet for me the results have been profound. I trust this will be helpful to you as well.

I have identified four emotions of life that are common to all of us. These emotions actually represent quite a bit of our experiences through the day. My goal has been to attempt to form a new habit by which I relate that emotion to God by talking with him about it.

I will start with the easiest one—*joy*. Paul says,

"Rejoice in the Lord always; again I will say, rejoice!" (Philippians 4:4). Is that characteristic of you? I wish I were there in my spiritual pilgrimage, but quite honestly I am not. But at least I can begin to rejoice in the Lord over the things that are naturally joyful. That is a start! Next time you experience a joyful situation—whether or not it seems to have anything to do with God—bring him into it by telling him about it. In a sense, "pray through" that emotion.

Before knowing anything about continual prayer I had a joyful experience skiing in the mountains of Colorado. I love to ski and had not had the opportunity to do it for a number of years. As I made my way down the slope I spontaneously blurted out, "Lord, this is great!" That might not sound too spiritual, but I was simply telling him what a great time I was having. The significance of this four-word prayer was that it changed my ski experience from my own activity to an activity with the Lord. No longer a "me" experience, but a "we" experience. When you share your joy with the Lord, he becomes involved in it with you.

The next time you experience joy, express it to God. Your joy becomes his as well, and the experience bonds you to him.

Another emotion I try to relate to the Lord is that of *boredom*. I cannot promise that you will experience joy today, but I'm sure that within the next few hours you will be bored. (I hope you are not feeling that right now!) Boredom offers a terrific opportunity to talk to God. It is as simple as saying, "Lord, I am bored, so here I am. What thoughts do you have for me today?" Take the boring times and share your thoughts with him. Do it when you're standing in line or waiting for the traffic to move.

Traffic lights irritate me beyond words. The very idea of a mechanical device demanding that I wait for it to change colors! It is especially irritating when I am late and there are no other cars coming from the other direction. I have attempted to take those boring, frustrating times to talk to God. It works! Boredom departs and I converse with the Lord!

Anger is another emotion that you can pray through and in so doing form a new habit that will lead to a continual conversation with God. This is more difficult, yet the results are life-transforming.

I am not advocating shaking your fist and yelling at God. By no means! But how much better to be honest than to turn your back on God and cease communicating with him. If you need to tell him your anger and even argue a bit, he can handle that. Skeptics may argue about God, but believers argue *with* God.

How practical is this? I will share a recent attempt on my part to pray through my anger. At our home we considered a project of replacing some old single-pane glass with new thermopane glass. Our consideration was hurried along when my son Christopher kicked a soccer ball through one of the old windows. After taking out all the old glass that was left over, I had what I thought to be a brilliant idea. I would take the old stuff to a glass shop, have it cut down to the appropriate sizes, and fit it to other windows of the house. That way I would have homemade storm windows.

The idea was basically a good one, except for the fact that the old glass had a way of getting broken as I transported it to and from the glass shop. If it survived the trip, I seemed to break it during installation. And if I was successful in getting it into place, it seemed that a sneeze was all it took to break it.

After many failures, I was still struggling to install the glass. I finally got to the last piece. I put it into place and it fit perfectly. I should have left it alone, but saw some paint on it and could not resist going for perfection. I withdrew the glass and began cleaning it with a scraper. I scraped a bit too hard. It cracked and fell into pieces at my feet. Upon hearing the crash, Katy and the kids no doubt expected to hear a verbal explosion. But instead I remembered my goal of attempting to pray through my anger. I looked at the pieces of broken glass—and I prayed! My prayer went like this: "Lord, I'm really ticked off!" That was it. At that point I thought of the entire comedy of errors of the homemade storm windows and began to laugh. My anger dissipated. I was communicating with the Lord and sharing the whole ridiculous experience with him.

The last emotion I will share is that of *depression.* One of the biblical names for the Messiah is *Counselor.* Christ is the one to whom we should bring our depression. I believe in the validity of some psychological therapy, but so often people seek a human counselor before they seek the Divine Counselor. When you are depressed you need to share with friends, your family, or a counselor. But place God at the top of your list. He is your primary Counselor.

David sought the Lord during times of depression, and many of the Psalms are his expressions of sorrow and melancholy. That is why the Book of Psalms is so helpful in times of depression. Reading the Psalms can lead us to share our own low times with God. Try it. Tell him exactly how you feel. He already knows, but he wants you to share it with him.

Once I received a phone call from a high school girl who had gone through a trauma at home. Her alcoholic father had tried to kill her mother. Fortunately, he was unsuccessful, and the police had taken him away. Her mother was with her at home but desired to be alone. Mary did not want any of us to come over, but she asked me if there were any verses in the Bible that told her what to do with her hurt and depression. At that time my knowledge of the Scriptures was quite limited, but I shared with her Philippians 4:6, 7, which tells us, "Don't worry about anything; instead, pray about everything; tell God your needs and don't forget to thank him for his answers. If you do this you will experience God's peace, which is far more wonderful than the human mind can understand. His peace will keep your thoughts and your hearts quiet and at rest as you trust in Christ Jesus" (TLB). I asked her to go to her room, shut the door, and tell God exactly how she felt—anger, depression, fear, and all.

The next day she called and said, "It works! I really felt his peace. It was unexplainable but true!"

My grandmother faced a depressing situation in her life, though she and my grandfather lived lives of intense devotion to Christ. My grandparents were mis-

sionaries in Brazil. There my father and his five brothers and one sister grew up together. I've heard many
stories about my grandparents even though I never
met them. All their children have commented about
the depth of their love for each other and for Christ. It
seemed that my grandmother had a continual conversation with God, for she seemed always to be praying.
Every day was an experience with God. Even moments
before her death they noticed her lips moving as she
talked with God.

In her earlier life in Brazil she spent most of her
time raising babies. Once as she was bathing her son,
Wilson, who was two years old, someone knocked at
the door. Grandmother left him in the tub to answer
the door. That seemed harmless enough because there
was only about one inch of water in the tub, and she
planned to be gone just a few minutes. But while she
was attending to the person who knocked, Wilson
managed to turn on the faucet. When Grandmother
returned, the tub was overflowing with water, and Wilson had drowned.

I cannot imagine a situation being more difficult
than this. Her reaction could have easily been: "God, I
sacrificed a lot to come to Brazil and tell others about
you. Why did you allow that person to come to the
door when he did? Why did you allow Wilson to turn
on the faucet? Why did I not get back sooner? Why did
this have to happen?" But this was not her response.
We cannot always have answers to suffering, and
Grandmother knew that.

Her attitude, I think, was this: "God, this is the

darkest hour of my life. I do not understand why this has happened, and it is the worst event of my life. But I am turning to you now. I trust you, and I know you will sustain me through this." What was the result of this openness with God? Someone overheard her speaking to her husband as they left the funeral service. She said to him, "Otis, what is this strange peace that I have?" He knew it to be the peace of Christ which transcends human understanding.

I wish I was more like my grandmother. I am a struggler just like you. I long to have a deeper relationship with God and to communicate with him constantly. We can all grow in that endeavor but must start at some point. Begin today! Begin sharing your thoughts with God. Turn off the many distractions in your life and talk with him. Tell him your joy, your boredom, your anger, your depression, and any other emotions or thoughts you have.

He is your Father and desires transparency with you. He responds to your prayer. He will impress you with his thoughts, his direction, and he will give you "the mind of Christ." He is simply waiting for you to turn to him in honesty, openness, and trust. And a continual conversation with him is what we desire so deeply: intimacy with God.

FOR REFLECTION

1. *What is the purpose of prayer?*

2. *What does Paul mean when he says, "Pray without ceasing"?*

3. *What did you learn from this chapter that will help your conversation with God the most?*

4. *What are some of the promises the Bible makes to those who pray?*

5. *With all the promises Jesus makes to those who pray, why do we do it so little?*

[1]Brother Lawrence and Frank Laubach, ed. Gene Edwards, *Practicing His Presence* (Augusta, Maine: Christian Books, 1973), p. 42.
[2]Ibid., 55.
[3]Ibid., 2, 3.
[4]Ibid., 32.

7

Gambling for Your Mind

What is happening to your mind as you go to the average movie, listen to popular music, and watch the standard prime-time TV shows?

Tear after tragic tear is shed before me as I talk to teenagers and young singles who suffer because they became influenced by what they were watching on TV and listening to via rock, and they began subconsciously to make decisions that hurt them deeply.

Of all scenes with sexual implications on TV "soaps," 92 percent involve single people or people who are not married to each other. (The average college student will have seen over one hundred thousand such scenes from TV alone since he turned thirteen.) Movies are even worse. Victor B. Cline conducted a revealing survey of the movies screened in theaters during a four-week period in a moderately conservative western city of twenty-five thousand. (This city did not have any "porno" movie houses. These were regular theaters.) The following is a summary of the sexual situations shown in the thirty-seven motion pictures screened during this period. (And don't forget, children were a part of the audiences.)

- Nudity—168 scenes
- Bed scenes with sexual connotations—49 scenes
- Seductive exhibition of the body—32 scenes
- Verbalizing of sexual interest or intentions—36 scenes
- Caressing another's sex organs while clothed—27 scenes
- Caressing another's sex organs while nude—21 scenes
- Undressing—34 scenes
- Explicit intercourse—19 scenes
- Suggested or implied intercourse—17 scenes
- Homosexual activities—11 scenes
- Oral-genital intercourse—7 scenes
- Rape—4 scenes
- Obscene gestures—4 scenes
- Masturbation—3 scenes
- Sexual sadomasochism—3 scenes

Remember, this is today's "acceptable" public entertainment. Has it become acceptable to you?

John Oates (of Hall and Oates) says, "Rock and roll is 99 percent sex."[1] When you listen to rock, most of the lyrics that talk about "sex being fun" and "sex being love" talk about doing it with a girlfriend or boyfriend, or even with someone else's wife, a relative, or someone of the same sex. Seldom do the songs say anything about purity or about the truly fulfilling sexual intimacy in marriage. And Rod Stewart says, "A happy home life, security, and in-laws aren't conducive to making rock and roll."[2]

Prince says it this way: "I realized that music could express what you were feeling and it started coming out in my songs—loneliness and poverty and sex." When asked about "Sister," a song about sex in the family, he said, "It is time to tell the truth."[3]

Steve Smith of Journey makes the plight of rock stars clear: "Rock stars are known for how many women they can take home or how many drugs they can consume."[4]

After a few years of disappointing record sales the Rolling Stones realized the way to become popular and sell their music to the American youth was through sex, rebellion, and Satan worship. "Now we're going after the mind," and so they did. "Sway" is a song about demon power, "Dancing with Mr. D" is about a graveyard romp with the devil and, "Sympathy for the Devil" is an anthem for many churches of Satan. The rest is history.

The average teenager will listen to over 150,000 "hits" by the time he graduates from high school. That is more influence than it took to brainwash the average soldier to Nazism during World War II.

So many students who are hooked on rock write off the influence by saying, "I don't even hear the words—I just listen to the music. It has no effect on me." I often hear the same story in the early stages of drinking, smoking pot, petting, etc. Most activities look harmless in the early stages. But I have seen so many harmful effects of sexually oriented rock—unwanted pregnancy, abortion, suicide, drug addiction,

Satan worship, and alcoholism. Rock doesn't *cause* these things, but the influence is there.

Too often we forget how much our minds are affected by the media. We forget that repetition is the best teacher, and repeated messages have a way of imbedding themselves in our consciousness.

See if you can finish these phrases that have been on TV many times over the past few years. "Two all beef patties, special sauce, lettuce, cheese, pickles, onions on a _____ ." "Reach out, reach out and touch _____ ." "Turn it loose, turn it loose, turn it loose _____ . Coors _____ Coors _____ Coors _____ ." "Hold the pickle, hold the lettuce, special orders _____ _____ _____ ."

Every time I play this memory game with a group of kids, every single one can finish the phrases. Of course, no one *studies* advertising. It just blows by during a commercial break. But it gets into your mind, doesn't it? And besides the relatively harmless ads for hamburgers and breakfast cereal, there are the ads that carry the message that physical beauty and material possessions are the really important things in life.

Knowing that you will become what you watch, what you listen to, and what you think about, you need to make a commitment to what you're going to allow into your mind. Commit yourself to the positive, not the negative.

God (who knows you intimately) and all the respected doctors and psychologists in the world agree that negative action begins with negative thought. Negative action brings about sin, hurt, and life without Jesus Christ. The choice is yours. It's the only mind you'll ever have.

The Apostle Paul understood the importance of fixing the mind on what is pure and noble. He wrote of this in 2 Corinthians 10:3-5:

For though we walk in the flesh, we do not war according to the flesh, for the weapons of our warfare are not of the flesh, but divinely powerful for the destruction of fortresses. We are destroying speculations and every lofty thing raised up against the knowledge of God, and we are taking every thought captive to the obedience of Christ.

Picture your mind as a fortress. In Bible times the fortress was the key to the protection of the city from the enemy, just as your eyes and ears are the fortress that protect your mind from Satan. The top of the wall of the city had a walkway where the soldiers stood to defend the wall. Your ability to turn your head, close your eyes, walk away, say no, turn off the stereo, etc., is your defense.

The battle plan of the invading army was to find a weak spot in the wall, break through or climb the wall, and conquer the city. Once the fortress was broken, there was much bloodshed and pirating in the city. No wonder the wall was built as strong as possible and manned with all of the strongest soldiers the city possessed.

Satan maintains his attack on your minds twenty-four hours a day. He wants to conquer the fortress and gain control over our lives by gaining entrance into our minds. His weapons are very effective. Skimpy bathing suits, pornographic magazines, movies, music, and TV are his most effective spears. When we drop our guard and allow his entrance, the battle rages inside our minds and the results are lust, immoral sex, alcohol and drug abuse, rebellion, abortion, suicide, and separation from God.

But we are not left without a powerful defense. God has equipped us with everything we need to defeat the enemy! Guys and girls, you can win the war!

"Our weapons are divinely powerful." We have God's weapons. As I fight the battle every day just like you, I've learned to depend on the weapons.

Only a few hours ago I saw a beautiful girl in tight blue jeans. Satan sent out a soldier to try to climb the wall of my mind. I knew that first thought could lead to lust which could lead to sexual sin (which I'd give my life to prevent).

Last night a TV advertisement interrupted a family show with a sexually implicit ad. Satan sent out a soldier.

One of my friends really hurt me behind my back by something he said and something he did. I wanted to get bitter. Satan sent out a soldier.

What do I do? What can you do?

Here's a course of action that works for me.

1. Flee—"Flee from youthful lusts" (2 Timothy 2:22). Run for your life! Get out of that situation as fast as you can. Never consciously go anywhere that you know will cause temptation to arise. If your friends are headed for a movie that you know is focused on sex, don't go.

2. Pray—"Pray that you may not enter into temptation" (Luke 22:40). I go straight to God. "Lord, I can't handle this alone. Give me wisdom to know the truth, give me courage to say no, give me weapons to defeat the enemy."

3. Memorize and personalize Scripture—"For the word of God is living and active and sharper than any two-edged sword" (Hebrews 4:12). Grab your sword. Turn your eyes and mind to God's Word. "Thy word I have treasured [memorized and prized] in my heart, that I may not sin against Thee" (Psalm 119:11).

I would have fallen into sin many times if I had not committed many chapters of God's Word to memory. Memorizing isn't very easy for me, but more than any other single thing it adds spears, soldiers, brick, and mortar to my fortress. As I identify Satan's soldier I immediately begin to meditate on God's Word, and I actually smile as that soldier is stopped dead in his tracks. Before I had God's Word treasured in my heart, that soldier often climbed the wall.

Personalize the Scriptures. As you read, study, memorize, and meditate on God's Word, put your name in the blanks. This love letter from God was written to you. Try inserting your name in these familiar verses.

"How blessed is _____ who does not walk in the counsel of the wicked, nor stand in the path of

sinners, nor sit in the seat of scoffers! But
_____'s delight is in the law of the Lord" (Psalm
1:1-3).

"Let the word of Christ richly dwell within
_____" (Colossians 3:16).

Begin a memory program today. Pick your favorite
passage or chapter and go for it! Even a small amount
of time and effort can produce a chapter a semester.
You'll be amazed in a few years how far you've come,
how tall your fortress is, and how safe your city has
become!

4. Develop a passion for a protected mind—Motivation is everything! Vince Lombardi said about the
great Redskin quarterback, Sonny Jergensen, "He always wanted to win so fiercely. All the great ones have
that."

You want to be a godly man or woman? You want to
know Christ and know how to really love your husband, wife, and children someday? You want a happy
life, a happy home, and a happy eternity? You want to
get free from your lust, your drugs, your guilt? Then
develop a passion for purity.

That want becomes a commitment to defeating the
enemy as soon as the enemy is recognized. Such a
commitment involves staying away from situations
where you know you'll be tempted. Thwart the enemy
by avoiding the "seedbeds" of temptation. Remember,
you don't easily avoid sex with your clothes off in the
backseat of a car. You avoid sex by dressing modestly
and refusing to fill your mind with the garbage you

can get from TV, films, and rock. You don't easily avoid drugs by watching as a joint is passed at a rock concert or party. You do it by staying as far away from such parties as possible. You'll never be an alcoholic if you never take another drink. You'll never be a gossip and a busybody if you never say another bad word about anyone. You'll never be a liar if you don't allow yourself to tell another lie.

You must be committed to protecting your mind if you want to know the joy of living the God first life!

FOR REFLECTION

1. How do negative thoughts progress into negative actions?

2. Why is it so vitally important to protect your mind?

3. What specific areas do you need to change in your life now?

4. Why is it so hard to give up rock, sexually oriented movies, etc., once you've started in on them?

---

[1]*Circus,* January 31, 1976, 39.
[2]*Circus,* October 17, 1978, 36.
[3]*Super Song Hits,* Summer 1985, 12.
[4]*Circus,* October 1982.

8

Here's the Beef—Obedience

I knew from the first night out that Debbie Jo, the girl I later married, was someone very different and very special. We had a blast on our dates! Because of our summer jobs we could only go out once a week for a few hours. I planned each date that first summer from start to finish with careful anticipation. We sailed, barbecued, water skied, played jacks in the laundromat, bowled, played pool (I lost), and did a string of pinball games. But mostly we laughed. I'd come home with a side ache from laughing with that girl.

One other thing we did—we ate. And could that 115-pound girl eat! Of all the dinners and cookouts we had, I'll never forget the night (our third date) that I packed a cooler with Dr. Pepper, watermelon, fresh corn-on-the-cob, and giant sirloin steaks. We put hickory limbs on our fire on the rocky beach of Table Rock Lake and cooked those steaks in butter. They were awesome! In fact, I couldn't finish mine. Not only did

Debbie Jo polish hers off quickly, she ate half of mine as well.

I still look forward to a good, lean steak cooked outside over a hickory fire. There's nothing quite like it. When you've had one of those, you know you've *really* eaten.

I pray this chapter will be a big filling steak to you. I hope you'll read it again and again. Pray for a moment right now and ask God to speak to you as we sit down for a steak dinner together.

Yes, here's the beef.

What One Thing Do These People I Know Have in Common?

• The man who left his wife and ten-year-old son and told me, "I did it because I didn't feel like I loved her anymore."

• The guy who spent the night with his girlfriend in the motel and rationalized to me, "We're going to get married someday anyway."

• The girl who listens to AC/DC (and a dozen other heavy metal groups) and says to me, "I don't study the words, so it doesn't affect me."

• The person who says, "I'll be there" and then doesn't bother to show up.

• The guy who walks out of a store with a stolen cassette tape stuffed in his pocket.

• The girl who sneaks out of her house to see her boyfriend late at night.

• You—when you eat too much or the wrong kind of food, are wasteful, gossip, get jealous over someone's clothes, use bad language, tell dirty jokes, and a million other varied examples.

All have one thing in common: disobedience to God.

Obedience, when properly understood and lived out, will change your life. It *is* the beef of the Christian faith.

In Christ you are free to do the right thing.

So if the Son [Christ] sets you free [from sin], you will be free indeed (John 8:36, NIV).

Through Christ Jesus the law of the Spirit of life set me free from the law of sin and death (Romans 8:2, NIV).

You have the ability to make and follow through with the right choices, choices that will bring you and those around you real love and happiness. You are free to obey God with your life.

It hasn't always been easy for me to be obedient to my parents or to God. I don't know many who can say that it isn't a struggle. A while back a verse that has made a difference in my life came alive to me:

"But thanks be to God that though you were slaves of sin, you became obedient from the heart" (Romans 6:17). Obedient from the heart! The heart is where obedience begins. The heart is the "quarterback" of the team. It's the "locomotive" of the train. It's the "roots" of the tree. It's the "seat" of authority. Your heart is where your life's direction is determined.

It is not easy to have an obedient heart. But God makes it possible.

One source of the power for obedience is the Holy Spirit, who indwells us as believers. I've grown to appreciate the last few words that Jesus shared with his closest friends the night before he died on the cross. He said to those who loved him most, "I will not leave you as orphans; I will come to you. After a little while the world will behold Me no more; but you will behold Me; because I live, you shall live also" (John 14:18, 19).

The disciples were confused. How could Jesus leave and still be with them? Jesus began to describe to them the Holy Spirit, who would come to live in a man's heart. He's the Spirit of truth. He's the one who makes you brave. He's the one who gives you the ability to live an obedient life. The Holy Spirit gives you the desire and power to live a life that you and God can feel good about.

I see the Holy Spirit as being a person who gives me the same type of direction that a seeing-eye dog gives to the blind man. The more I follow him, the more I realize the need that I have to hang on tight and to allow him to keep each step planted firmly on the pathway that he wants me to go. As I look off the path I see a tragic world of divorce, crime, jealousy, fighting, adultery, fornication, child abuse, lust-oriented media, and I say to him, "Lord, keep me right in the middle of the path." If I'll hold on to him and follow his guiding, he will keep me there.

The Holy Spirit gives me the power and the ability to live a life obedient to Christ. You'd think I was crazy if I brought you over to a new Firebird that I just bought, and as I showed it off to you I began to push it down the driveway. You'd scream at me, "Get in and start the engine." What if I said, "Engine, what's that?" and I continued pushing it along? You'd run over and say, "Hey, look here," then you'd open the hood of the car. And I would say, "What's that for?" You'd say, "You crazy? Get in and I'll show you."

As you turned the ignition and the engine revved up, I'd be amazed as the car raced off with power to burn.

A pretty silly thought, but it's not any sillier than a guy or girl who tries to live his life on his own power. Here we have the Holy Spirit, God within, giving us power to live an obedient life! And we try to get out and push the car and live it on our own.

I read not long ago about a school that burned down in Texas. When they rebuilt the school, they put in an elaborate set of fire sprinklers in the ceiling. They were sure the school would never burn down again. But it happened. The second time the school burned down, the engineers rushed to the scene; when questioned about why the fire sprinklers didn't stop the fire, they went over to the valve that led to the water system and realized that the valve had never been turned on! That was probably one of the biggest mistakes that's ever been made in construction. But it's an even bigger mistake when you or I try to live our lives obedient to God without depending upon the power of the Holy Spirit. When you realize that the will of the flesh is more powerful than anything except God's Spirit, you'll begin to depend upon him.

The Holy Spirit is called the *parakletos*. At the time the New Testament was being written, a *parakletos* was a man who was called into a defeated group of soldiers to put courage in their hearts. The Holy Spirit will give you the courage to live an obedient life, even when the peer pressure is indescribable.

The Holy Spirit is the *Comforter*. That doesn't mean the one who makes it easy, but it means the one who enables a wavering person to be brave. He gives us abundant bravery as we attempt to live our lives obedient to God.

No wonder Paul said in 2 Corinthians 9:15, "Thanks be to God for His indescribable gift!" I think about the feeling I had inside the first time I saw my first little daughter born in the hospital. I could only say as she squirmed inside her crib and tears streamed down my face, "God, thank you for this indescribable gift." The Holy Spirit is so much greater.

If we have this indescribable gift, why do we sin? When we sin, we grieve the Holy Spirit. To grieve the Holy Spirit means to bring him pain. This can happen through deceit, doubt, distress, worry, bitterness, or unclean thoughts, words, or actions. When we grieve the Holy Spirit we take the power away from our ability to live the obedient life. The Holy Spirit is a person, and we can hurt him just like we can hurt anyone else.

When we sin, we also quench the Holy Spirit. We quench the Holy Spirit in the same way we quench a fire. The first way to put out a fire is to withdraw the fuel. The fuel that we give the Holy Spirit is our prayer time, our study time, our time of fellowship, and our time of witnessing to others. The second way to quench a fire is by spraying water or a fire extinguisher on the flame. We extinguish the flame of the Holy Spirit by sinning willfully in things such as lying, putting anything into our bodies that is harmful, or doing anything that would cause someone else to stumble.

But sin doesn't have to get the better of us. We can willingly give the Spirit control, letting him fill our lives. To be filled with the Holy Spirit means to be under the authority of, under the control of, under the influence of, and empowered by the Holy Spirit. You can be filled with the Holy Spirit today if you

1. desire it with all your heart,
2. confess all known sins,
3. repent and turn away from those sins,
4. surrender your life to the control of the Holy Spirit, and
5. continue moment by moment, day by day to live under this control and authority.

It's a whole lot like a marriage relationship. Fourteen years ago I looked Debbie Jo in the eye and said, "Debbie Jo, I give you my life, I give you my purity, I give you everything that I have," and I give her that 365 days out of the year. She and I enjoy a dynamic marriage relationship. When you give that kind of commitment to the Holy Spirit, you will enjoy a relationship of obedience to Jesus Christ.

You can live an obedient life to Christ when you live it by the power of his *grace.* As I do something right, I've come to realize it's not a personal victory, but it's a victory for God. I've learned to give credit where credit is due. An electric lamp doesn't glow by itself; it glows because of the electricity that comes from the outlet. The source of my obedience is not myself, but God's grace. God, knowing that we're unable to be obedient on our own power, went all the way to the cross to give us his grace so that we can obey his loving truth. God's grace is explained in this verse: "The wages of sin is death, but the free gift of God is eternal life in Christ Jesus our Lord" (Romans 6:23).

Because of grace, there is no legalism. The relationship between God and man is no longer the relationship of creditor and debtor, of judge and defendant; through Jesus, it's an acceptance of God's grace and a commitment to living in his love. The motivation for right living is no longer fear of punishment. The motivation is this unconditional love, which should fill us with gratitude. When I realize that God loves me just like I am, it makes me want to be obedient to this love.

During your next daily quiet time, look up the following Bible verses and begin to discover how great it is to be an obedient Christian.

- 1 Peter 1:22—Obedience purifies the soul.
- Romans 8:1, 2—Obedience is the key to freedom.
- Joshua 1:8—Obedience is the price of success.
- James 1:25—Obedience is the price of blessing.
- Matthew 5:19—Obedience is the price of greatness.
- 1 Samuel 15:22—Obedience is better than sacrifice.
- Hebrews 5:8; Philippians 2:8—Jesus Christ expressed total obedience in his life. He would pay any price for obedience. His obedience had no limits.
- Matthew 7:21—Obedience makes Jesus the Lord of your life.
- John 15:10—Obedience is the vital element necessary for abiding with Christ.

In John 14:15, Jesus says, "If you love Me, you will keep My commandments." How much do you love Jesus today? When I ask Christians if they love Jesus, they will almost always answer yes. But if we believed the words in John 14:15, we would express our love through obedience. If the most precious thing in the world is our relationship with Jesus Christ, then we will realize the need to be obedient to him in every area of life. How much do you love Jesus today? Do you want to tell him that you love him by the way you live?

Therefore everyone who hears these words of Mine, and acts upon them, may be compared to a wise man, who built his house upon the rock. And the rain descended, and the floods came, and the winds blew, and burst against that house; and yet it did not fall, for it had been founded upon the rock. And everyone who hears these words of Mine, and does not act upon them, will be like a foolish man, who built his house upon the sand. And the rain descended, and the floods came, and the winds blew, and burst against that house; and it fell, and great was its fall (Matthew 7:24-27).

These great verses give us the key to a life that can stand during the storms of our growing-up years. Is the pressure at school great? Is the pressure at home great? Why do we Christians fall apart when the storms begin to brew in our lives? The reason we fall is the same reason a home that's built on a weak foundation falls. The house that is built on a firm foundation will never fall in a storm.

It's tough to be a Christ-like man or woman. It's tough to raise a unified, happy family. It's tough to live a life that will make things happen for the kingdom of God on earth. But if your life is built upon the solid rock foundation of obedience to Jesus Christ and all that he does, you will not fail. When you look back at your years on this planet, you and Jesus will smile as he says to you, "Well done, faithful servant. How pleased I am to have you in my eternal family."

FOR REFLECTION

1. Why is the Holy Spirit called "the Helper"?

2. Why is being "filled with the Spirit" a moment-by-moment commitment to being obedient to God?

3. How important is it to God that we be obedient to his Word?

4. How much of God's Word does he desire that we obey?

5. How important is it to you to keep God's commandments?

6. What percent of God's commandments do you keep?

7. If your love for Jesus is expressed by your obedience, how much do you love him?

9

The Measure of Greatness

A tragic childhood encounter with polio had left Cathy's face distorted, mouth twisted, and throat permanently paralyzed. Her speech was broken and difficult to understand. But a sweetness and purity beamed tenderly from a beautiful pair of blue eyes. When her all-important senior prom arrived, she had never been asked for a date. Her fate as a social outcast was obvious. Nobody would ask Cathy to our prom—well, nobody except David, the president of our student council!

David was tall, gentle, and kind. He wasn't an athlete of any variety, but his popularity increased as his unselfish heart grew to be appreciated on our high school campus of four hundred students. When David showed up with Cathy at the prom, we all felt like giving him a standing ovation! He wasn't there to get attention. He simply believed that Cathy's need for love and acceptance was more important than the ridicule he might receive for bringing her. He didn't get any ridicule. He only received respect.

Who took the school beauty to that prom? I don't recall. Who took the homecoming queen? I forgot that, too. I don't recall my own date, but David is in my personal Hall of Fame. At the prom Cathy was noticed by another fine neighborhood friend named Jimmy, who recognized Cathy's splendid potential. Her dreams were fulfilled two years later when Jimmy asked Cathy for her hand in marriage. David was, I think, a truly great person.

So is my father. Every Monday and Friday the garbage collectors came to the back door of our central Texas home. Every Monday and Friday my father met the men at the door with a beaming smile over cups of steaming hot coffee and warm buttery sweet rolls. If the president of the United States had come to our door, he would have received no finer greeting from my dad. One day a very poor man in our town encountered my dad. In a casual conversation with the man, Daddy noticed that the man had on a pair of rundown, soleless shoes. Without much ado Daddy stooped down, unlaced his own shoes, and traded shoes with the man. Not a day goes by that I don't see Daddy doing similar things for the folks he meets. (And I'm sure my dad would agree that my mother is even MORE consistently thoughtful than he is! What a pair of attractive parents I have!)

Jesus said over and over that "your measure of greatness is shown by the depth in your care for others."

Today we have tall churches, giant youth groups, and stacks of Bibles. For sure, no people in any place at any time have ever had more opportunities for spiritual growth than we have. Christian radio, Christian TV, Christian music, and Christian books are everywhere. But since so much is happening around us, why isn't more happening *through* us? Are we content to be *passive* Christians? (Perhaps the real question is, *Can* you be a passive Christian?)

The most consistently successful football coach to ever enjoy the profession was Bud Wilkinson of the Oklahoma Sooners. He once remarked, "Modern day football is twenty-two men on the field who desperately need rest and twenty-two thousand people in the stands who desperately need exercise."

Our religion is similar. We're a generation of spectators when it comes to applying the love we study in the Bible. We like to go to church, listen to Christian music, and read Christian books. But it isn't enough. James puts it this way: "Do not merely listen to the word. . . . Do what it says" (James 1:22).

The heart of the Christian life is not made in Sunday school, at retreats, or in a youth group meeting. It only begins there. That's where we get the fuel. Our real walk with Christ takes place wherever people are hurting and starving for love. And this walk with Christ—doing the Word, not just hearing it—means taking the hard road. Talking to the school cheerleader is easy. Talking to the school bum is the real test of character. Thanking your parents with a smile when they give you the car can be done by any sixteen-year-old. But love is expressed when you smile and say, "I'll be happy to" as your parents express their desire that you come straight home after the movie or, if you're in college, you're asked to come

home for spring break rather than joining your fraternity brothers on a trip to Ft. Lauderdale.

A teenage girl sent me this story in a letter last winter. I don't know who wrote it, but I believe it is worth
sharing with you.

*Billy was sitting on a park bench, enjoying the beautiful flowers
and joys of springtime. A man approached and sat down on the
bench. Soon they began to talk. First they discussed the weather,
later the Dodgers and Yankees, then each made a few comments
about the building being erected down the street . . . until there
was a moment of silence between them.*

*Shortly the man spoke almost as if intruding upon the silence.
He asked Billy what he would wish for if he were given three
wishes which would be fulfilled regardless of what they were. Billy thought for a moment and then he said, "First, I would want
to know God . . . and Jesus, too; second, I would want everyone
to know Jesus; and . . . and third, I would want Paul, my blind
friend, to see again. These would be my three wishes."*

*Upon hearing these words, the man seemed puzzled, if not as-
tonished. He paused a moment, smiled, and after a moment's
hesitation walked away giving a slight nod.*

*Billy could not understand why the man acted so strangely.
He thought for awhile, shrugged his shoulders, picked up his
crutches, and hobbled home.*

Such behavior as Billy's would indeed puzzle some
people. Most folks are so unaccustomed to unselfish-
ness that they assume a crippled person would ask,
first, to be made physically whole. But we should be
happy to puzzle people in this way.

A missionary to a very poor nation in South Africa
made a tremendous impression on a young African
boy when she taught the boy how to read and write.
When Christmastime rolled around, the boy was dis-
tressed because he had no money to buy a present for

the missionary. An idea came to his mind. About a two-and-a-half days' walk up the ocean was an inlet beach where people often found a rare and very beautiful seashell. The boy began his journey in his ragged old clothes. Five days later he returned home with his prize find in his pocket. He rushed to the teacher's house to deliver his treasure.

The teacher knew the value of the shell. Her eyes showed amazement as she received the cherished Christmas present.

"Why did you go to such trouble for me?" the teacher asked.

The boy's reply was brief and heartfelt: "Much love."

"I know you love me," the teacher persisted, "but you walked five days to get me this lovely shell."

The boy's humble reply echoes in my heart every day, "Much love, long walk."

Much love, long walk. Being kind is a long walk around your own selfish desires. Treating a girl with respect on a date often requires a long walk around a guy's own desire for instant gratification. Saying "I love you" to your mom or dad requires a long walk to your storehouse of smiles and pleasant attitudes. But the trip is worth it!

Jimmy Dodd is a tall, dark-haired friend of mine from a large high school in Kansas. He became a Christian during his high school days and had a desire to share his new faith. After much prayer and thoughtful consideration he obtained the addresses and birthdays of everyone in high school, and he personally sent each one a birthday card with a personal handwritten note telling each amazed schoolmate about his relationship with Jesus Christ. Many were touched. Much love, long walk.

Each year in our summer camp we ask our teenage campers and college staff to write their parents a love letter. Asking for anything or complaining about anything are against the rules. This letter is only to thank them for all they have done. It is an expression of love for the two people who made life possible.

The parents, deeply touched, often write back. For many the "I love you, Mom and Dad" in the letter hasn't been expressed in years. One lonely, divorced dad answered his daughter's letter. She came running to me. The father had said, "I love you" to her. He hadn't told anyone those three words in over four years! Maybe no one had showed him how!

Much love, long walk!

I know three teenage boys whose mom is in a wheelchair, paralyzed for life. Her husband left her after her tragic accident. The driveway to their house was eroded and the house was in great disrepair. As I entered the house I picked up a beer can which was lying discarded on the porch. The oldest boy came to the door. The other two, sprawled out on couches, were watching television. The mother was propped up in bed studying her Bible. Her eyes flooded with tears as she expressed her unceasing love for her husband and her prayers that her "I'm First" sons would change. Looking around her room I noticed a screen falling off the window. The result of "I'm Number One" living had been handed down from father to sons. Someday, when they have their own sons, perhaps they will understand.

Jesus said, "If anyone wants to be great, let him be servant of all." That's his offer to you today. Let your imagination wander for a moment to those around you—your family, your friends, your teammates, and others. What can you do to be an "I'm Third" person toward them right now?

FOR REFLECTION

1. What made David different? Why did he take Cathy to the prom?

2. Do you know anyone like David? How do you feel about him?

3. Why does "much love" often require a "long walk"?

4. What does it mean to "love your neighbor as you love yourself"?

5. Name some specific people in your life who need more of this kind of love from you. How can you put this Christ-like love into practice?

10

Take the Leadership Challenge

*W*hat comes to mind when you think of the word *leader?* I used to think of a leader as someone decked out in his army uniform, with medals on his chest and a sword hanging from his belt. In my mind he was pointing at the enemy, with his arm outstretched as he boldly screamed, "Charge, men! Attack the enemy!" This kind of tough-as-nails leader commands respect and helps draw out courage in others. He's an "out-front" person who doesn't let someone else decide what path he'll follow.

As I've grown to understand the life of teenagers, I've been tremendously impressed with the need for solid student Christian leaders on the junior high, high school, and college campus. But the only sword you need as a Christian leader is a growing knowledge of the Word of God. Medals and a uniform aren't absolutely necessary either. It's the Christ-filled heart deeply planted that equips you for the great challenge of leadership! (Like the tough-as-nails leader I mentioned in the first paragraph, the Christian leader is able to take the initiative and not always follow the dictates of the crowd.)

I've grown to admire an outstanding college quarterback who is on our sports camp summer staff. Many Saturday afternoons I've watched him on TV leading his team with accurate passing and swift, determined running. Kent is a respectable leader. He believes drugs and drinking are detrimental to his health and his Christian witness, so he consistently refrains from partaking of liquor or entering bars. As Kent went on to his senior year, his coach called him into his office. He realized Kent was quite distinct in his social habits from the majority of his teammates. Kent was amazed when his coach told him to "loosen up, have a few drinks with the guys, and relate to the team on their level." Kent retained his polite nature as he made it very clear to his coach that he would continue to live out his convictions and wouldn't change his standards to please anyone. He is still starting. His team is still winning football games.

A nineteen-year-old friend of mine is an attractive model in Paris, France. If you think it is hard to be a Christian teenage leader in America, try it in France! Here's a letter from her:

Dear Joe,

Bonjour! It was so good to hear from you. Things got a lot more complicated after I wrote you. God taught me so much! It's through those rough times that one learns so much! People over here have definitely seen the difference in me. I've had the opportunity to witness to some of them and it's so exciting to see them discover God!

Many people try to bring me down for my convictions. If they only knew it was the neatest thing ever! Some people just can't imagine a true God. Joe, I just don't want to see any of them miss out on the most wonderful experience in life. I don't know how they can manage without God. Man, I know I couldn't.

> *Love,*
> *Rebecca*

Last spring I spoke to a group of high school students in Kona Kuai, Hawaii. I was fascinated by the beauty, the sweet-smelling leis everyone was constantly putting around your neck, the white sand, black sand, and even green sand beaches.

The teenagers there were missing the beauty. I learned as I talked to kids that this school in Kona had the highest teen pregnancy rate in America and the number one cash crop was "Kona gold" (local marijuana).

I met one boy who was different. He was happy, outgoing, athletic. He was a leader. Here's what he wrote me after our visit:

Dear Joe,

Just wanted to write and let you know how things are in Hawaii. Kona is changing. I see a lot of new faces in school and in church. The church is gaining many "sheep" and losing the "goats." More and more I feel God's call to be a "sheep." I have now incorporated praise during my Bible study. The effect it's had on my life is unbelievable. No longer do I drag through my days. God has given me a joy that is ineffable. When I walk through the halls I just want to stop those guys that are "stoned" and give them a piece of my heart. I want to share! I've never felt this way before. In times past, I was scared to share. Now I find myself having to wait for God's leadership.

Also, I'm learning that I don't always have to say something. The Lord is working through my actions. I never realized how many people knew me until just this year. God has really impressed upon me how many lives I affect. Anyway, I've really been trying to get my act together this year because the call is strong. I don't want to be sitting around rocking in my rocking chair when the Lord comes.

My life has turned around so fast that many commented including friends and coaches. Since then, life has been a joy instead of a drag.

Aloha,
Todd

When you compromise your standards to fit into what's happening around you, you're not only letting God and yourself down, you're letting your friends down. Love them enough to be a leader! Care enough to set a new pace. When the locker room talk gets off-color or cutting, when fellow students are getting ripped apart with gossip, when parents or school authorities are getting disrespect, when someone's purity is at stake, when someone suggests a keg party . . . STAND UP! Stand up and be a leader.

Listen to this Ft. Worth, Texas, high school girl who acted in the role of a Christian leader:

The ski camp was so good for me. It gave me a chance to spend quality time with friends. I realized that I had a wonderful opportunity to reveal to ten of my closest friends the love of my life. These were people I spent time with, went to school with, and in one moment I could make or break the fact that Christ was the most important thing in my life. I decided that the opportunity was too great to pass up! It was scary, but God really blessed me that night. Traci accepted Christ! She told me later, "You know, Alexis, I've had a lot of questions and I was pretty sure that you could answer them, but I was always scared to ask. After you talked tonight, though, all my fears were calmed. I'm not sure why I asked you to talk, but am really glad that I did!"

The secret is simply this, "Christ in you" (Colossians 1:27).

A buddy of mine from California named Steve Haas took the leadership challenge two summers ago. He believed he could do "all things" through Jesus Christ who lived in his heart as a believer. Steve was tired of talking about love and talking about the hurting world. He desired to *act* on that love and lead those around him into that starving world.

He and a friend took the "Christ in you" principle to a starvation refugee camp near Bangkok, Thailand, just across the Cambodian (Kampuchean) border. He wrote me of his experience.

After a month of orientation duties within the camp compound my working partner, Russ, and myself were given permission to set up a recreational program for orphaned children, mostly of teen age, who spent most of their time alone due to the lack of opportunities in the camp. These were the forgotten ones, and except for the occasional visit from relief agency volunteers, these children remained alone. Most had witnessed atrocities, often of family members as they had fled their war-torn home-lands. To survive, most had built emotional walls that would pro-vide a strong defense lest anyone try and hurt them again.

Being rather brash and headstrong, Russ and I figured we could provide for these persons' needs by our own intelligence and creativity. After all, we were both athletes, with experience in youth programming, so what more could we need?

The fact is that four days later we were both bemoaning the fact that we had ever taken on such a responsibility. We had tried hugging kids, playing with them, smiling at them, touching them, and all we had to show for it all was a multitude of fake smiles, forlorn little faces, and no touch in return. Was it too much to ask that someone smile back when they are smiled at, or squeeze in return when a hug or handshake is given? Our self-righteous frustration dissolved into tears.

In our quickness to be proven a success, we had forgotten to include Christ in the whole affair. Our goal was to reap the fruits of a successful program, to hear the voice of our superiors say "Well done," to give affection and feel it in return. We realized that these were not wrong motives in and of themselves, but that Christ wanted us for more than this. God's plan not only could break down the barriers these children had erected, but bring them wholeness if we were but willing and open vessels for use. Both of us determined that from that moment onward we would concentrate on seeing Christ in the hearts and lives of these troubled youngsters. No longer would we be dependent on the outward signs of affection, which they might never give, but that it would be Christ in us that would touch these people to new life.

Let it be known that things remained as they were for almost three weeks. Both of us would return home emotionally wiped out, only finding strength through a daily feeding on God's Word. It remained as usual until, during one of our early morning walks, one of the Vietnamese children Russ worked with greeted him by taking hold of his hand. This may seem like small reward for the amount of labor that had gone into our recreational program, but you would have never guessed by the beaming smiles that lighted up our faces. Daily, more began to open up, to share their pain, to touch and receive touch unashamed. They had been touched, but not with our touch, for ours had given out after only four days. These beautiful people had been touched by the love of Christ, when words and ethnic backgrounds could not communicate.

From the world's perspective, it's sheer foolishness to think that the living presence of Christ can really make that much difference in a world that seems bent on its own destruction. But as Christians, we have the manual of life open for us to read and understand. It states there that Christ wants to make a difference in your environment through you, with his power and love. It's his plan of salvation, and it will work whether you are a part of the process or not. The question is, Will it be Christ in you?

Under grace,
Steve

Paul said, "Imitate me as I imitate Christ." That's not arrogance. That's the cry of a leader, someone determined to do great things and to encourage others to do so. President Roosevelt once spoke of this determination: "It is far better to dare mighty things even though checked by failure than to take ranks with those spirits who neither enjoy much or suffer much because they know not victory or defeat."

Jesus had a passion to bring the world to God. John the Baptist had a passion to pave the way. Paul had a passion to take the gospel to the world no matter what the cost. In the Book of Acts we read about one of my greatest heroes, a man named Stephen. As the Jews prepared to stone him to death, Stephen used the opportunity to proclaim the eternal salvation of Jesus Christ. While the stones began to fly, Stephen looked up and saw Jesus in heaven, standing by God as if to give this giant-hearted man a standing ovation while Stephen passed out of this life into eternity. Have you ever felt like Stephen? When your friends want you to compromise, think about this.

In the Civil War a certain young sergeant named Jerome Davis was the color guard for the North. His assignment was to plant the American flag upon a hill as his regiment took the new territory from a very competitive Rebel army. Sergeant Davis charged through the heavy barrage of musket balls, cannonballs, and black powder, his eyes fixed firmly on the summit he was assigned to take. Suddenly he noticed that his regiment was retreating and he was alone. As he planted the Union flag into the hill, a corporal screamed forward to the sergeant, "Sergeant Davis, bring the colors back to the regiment!" Without a moment's hesitation Jerome Davis yelled back, "The colors are where they're supposed to be! Bring up the regiment!" Davis knew he was where he was supposed to be.

Christians should know where they're supposed to be—spiritually, morally, mentally. We have an unwavering standard to follow: Jesus Christ. He is the same today as he was yesterday and will be forever. His standards do not change. He knows what brings true love. He knows the source of happiness and peace and satisfaction. As those around you retreat into the distance of sexual permissiveness, drinking, drugs, rebellion, etc., plant God's flag where it is supposed to be and bring up the regiment!

It has been said that you can take the Texan out of Texas, but you can't take Texas out of the Texan. Once a Texan always a Texan! I'm not sure what it is about that giant piece of real estate that develops so much patriotism and allegiance, but I've got to admit it is effective. I live in the Ozark Mountains of southern Missouri now, but I'm still a Texan at heart.

No single event has affected that exciting state's history more profoundly than the Battle of the Alamo. Every little kid in Texas can tell you the details of the conflict. Hollywood captured the grueling thirteen-day battle several years ago and properly backed up our childhood tales of Davy Crockett, Jim Bowie, William Travis, and their bigger-than-life commitment to the independence of the State of Texas from Mexico.

As the battle intensified and the now famous 180 heroes dug in to defend the mission against Santa Anna's mighty army, the thought that no American would walk out of the battle to tell the Alamo story set into the small band of defenders with grim reality. The admirable Colonel William B. Travis called his band of soldiers together. He let their sure fate of death be known. Then he drew his sword and struck a line into San Antonio's dust as he boldly proclaimed their life-and-death choice. "We're buying precious time for Sam Houston to prepare the Texas army for the upcoming battle for Texas' independence. Every day we hold out against Santa Anna is twenty-four invaluable hours of training. Our effort will be known in history as the difference between Sam Houston's victory or defeat!" And then Colonel Travis looked squarely into the eyes of his 179 men and said, "In the final days of this battle, every man who stays with me will surely die." The pages of history ring with his final declaration, "You who wish to die like heroes and patriots, come over to me and step over this line. You who choose to leave, stay where you are." At first, no one dared a step. Then one brave soul stepped across the line—then there were two, three, four, and more. When Crockett made his move he was joined by more than a dozen. Poor Jim Bowie was so sick that he had to be carried across on a stretcher. Soon 178 men joined Travis and made the choice to stand, to defend, to die. Only one could not accept the challenge.

As they fell to the overpowering Mexican cannon and muskets, their cry built a momentum that would soon be heard across America, "Remember the Alamo! Remember the Alamo!"

The men who stepped across the line didn't live to hear "Remember the Alamo!" They had no real assurance the U.S. would win the war with Mexico. But William Travis knew he was doing the right thing by staying on to fight. So did the men who joined him. They stepped across the line—not because it was the easy choice, but because it was right. Travis was a great leader because he led the group in making the right choice.

Will you step across the line today? Will you make a commitment in prayer right now to set down standards by the standards in God's Word and bring your friends, family, teammates, and dates with you? Dare to be a leader! God will give you all the power you need to follow through with your commitment.

FOR REFLECTION

1. Why are solid Christian leaders so rare?

2. Think of a person whom you respect as a leader. Pinpoint one outstanding quality that impresses you about this person.

3. What type of leader is easiest to follow?
   a. One who tells you what to do?
   b. One who shows you what to do?
   c. One who does both?
Why?

4. What qualities of leadership did Jesus Christ display in his life?

5. Why was he the greatest leader of all time?

11

What's in It for Me?

"*I*f it feels good, do it!" The bumper sticker proclaimed the philosophy of the late twentieth century. According to this philosophy, you can't listen to parents and preachers and go around pleasing everyone. Just do what feels right and you'll be cool.

Jesus says, "Love your neighbor as you love yourself." The Apostle Paul elaborated on this in Philippians 2:3-5:

Do nothing from selfishness or empty conceit, but with humility of mind let each of you regard one another as more important than himself; do not merely look out for your own personal interests, but also for the interests of others. Have this attitude in yourselves which was also in Christ Jesus.

What a formula for real life happiness! I urge you to memorize it and ask God to help you put it into effect in your life today.

Why? Because the effects of self-centered living are painfully obvious.

Last fall I was asked to speak at two football banquets. One team had lost all ten of their games. The other had won nine and lost one. Both teams had some good athletes. Neither had exceptional talent. Each had a dedicated coaching staff.

Before the first banquet I asked some of the players of the losing team if anyone did drugs. One player said, "Not many—only about 70 percent!" Another player and the team captain assured me it was more like 80 percent. As I spoke to the team, their parents, dates, and school administration, I charged them with the responsibility for their miserable season. No wonder they couldn't beat anyone. No wonder the school spirit was almost nil. (I later learned that all teachers in the school are absolutely forbidden to mention God in any way. No Christian counseling is available and no Christian clubs are allowed on campus.) The students look out for their own spiritual needs as best they can. The drugs, the spirit, and the season record underline God's truth. Without a commitment to love each other, defeat is felt on every front.

Three weeks later I drove to the winning team's banquet. I wondered if it would be the same as the first one. As I entered the banquet hall, I sensed a great difference in atmosphere. Enthusiasm and cheers filled the room, and these were more than victory cheers—the team had *lost* their last game only a few days before! These were cheers from the hearts of players and coaches and cheerleaders and pep club girls who were committed to loving each other. The captain described to me the high percentage of committed Christians on the team. He knew of no more than 10 percent who did pot or other drugs. Only one out of five ever drank.

It's true that not every "I'm First" team will be 0-10. Every "I'm Third" team will surely not end up with a 9-1 record. But God's unshakable truth remains: When one member of a team (a family, a dating couple, a school) looks out strictly for his own interests, everyone suffers. When one member is built up, the whole team shares the glory.

Ironically, a month later I ate lunch on the training table of our nation's pre-season pick for the Number One NCAA college football team. Their season was most disappointing. They didn't even win their conference title, nor did they end up in the Top Ten nationally. A big, strong (in body *and* in spirit!) interior lineman was my host at lunch. "Greg, why," I asked, "did y'all play so poorly? What made your team fall apart?"

"We're so selfish," he replied. "Everyone's playing for himself. And many of our team leaders were going out at night and getting rowdy."

"You mean drinking during season?" I queried.

"Yes, the night before the game even. But it was more than that. The drinking and partying hurt, but that was just indicative of how selfish everyone was. Football is a team sport. You've got to sacrifice for your teammates. If that means staying in at night or if it means not talking trash about anyone else behind his back, that's what you do."

What works on a football team also works in a marriage.

Currently, one of America's favorite professional athletes is going through a very hurtful divorce from his lovely wife. Both parties are crushed. They sought a marriage counselor and each told his side of the story. After their time together, the counselor said,

"Larry [names changed], you and Diana are almost impossible. You are both so self-centered and so intensely interested in what YOU want that your marriage will never make it. You'll never be able to go on as husband and wife until you can change your basic attitude and begin to put the other's needs and desires ahead of your own."

A suicidal girl came to me in desperation a month ago. She had experienced tragedy after tragedy. She felt like she was at the very bottom and sought to live no longer. As I sensed her acknowledged love for life, I gave her a challenge. The challenge included twenty-five chewable vitamin C tablets. She was to chew one a day, but only after she had done something very, very special to someone who was dear to her. She began with a letter to her parents expressing her love and appreciation. Then she moved to teachers and friends around her. Day after day she took her "pill" as she brought sunshine to someone else's life with an unexpected kindness. Last week I saw a beautiful brown-eyed girl with a new twinkle in her eyes and an unfamiliar smile glued to her face. "I'm doing a lot better now," she glowed as she spoke. "The vitamins are gone—every one of them." I don't think she needed the vitamin C tablets, but I knew she needed the love and self-respect that came to her as she spent each day planning her next "I'm Third" adventure.

I find that if I make every effort from the time I wake up in the morning until the time I go to sleep at night to do everything possible to make my wife, my four splendid kids, and my friends feel good about themselves, my world gets happier. There's more to sharing love—more sheer enjoyment—more laughter and just plain fun—than anything I could get on my own.

If you cast out the crumbs of love, you get a loaf of love in return! If you cast out the crumbs of "I don't care" and "I'm Number One," that's what comes back!

I've known for several years the eighteen-year-old who wrote this letter. She always did what felt good at the moment. She refused to listen to her parents and really didn't care about anything except her immediate desires. Now she's realizing the results.

Dear Joe,

Everything you said about how people go on my past record really hits home. All of a sudden it's senior year and I'm just now seeing how bad I hurt myself. My grades show it. I regret a lot of things now. Right now I'm trying to pull my grades up, but one semester can't make up for the past three years of high school. Getting turned down by a college isn't what's bothering me. It is the fact that I could have done so much better.

What a contrast there is between the smiles "I'm Third" living brings and the sadness that is fostered by the "I'm First" life-style. Letters like the following are not rare in my mailbox.

Dear Joe,

I am a twenty-year-old young lady who has lived the past year of her life with only regrets to remember. Since a young age (twelve), I have been a Christian. My fellowship with God was so wonderful that all I wanted to do was serve him. His inner joy and peace was so fantastic! By eighteen, though, the pressure to date around increased and finally I compromised and went out with the wrong guy. No big deal, right? Wrong! One compromise really leads to another. Don't misunderstand—the guy started out as a sweet, caring person! Unfortunately, he didn't end up that way. I wasn't happy in the situation, but people made me feel like it was right. I was pretty dumb. Anyway, by my nine-teenth birthday (actually on my birthday) Brian made his move. I compromised and gave in; he got what he had wanted all along. Later he laughed and said he thought he had been pretty smooth, not rushing into anything. A year-long relationship—all hands off—then that! And I lost my life! I hated myself; I couldn't even look at myself. I turned away from God, and the louder he called, the farther I ran. I felt my heart break into pieces. The guilt was so horrible that I stayed plastered most of the time, but it didn't help. I really wanted to die.

But now as I read Looking for Love *the second time through and have heard you speak, I finally have received and accepted God's love and forgiveness.*

I'm glad that some of these sad letters have happy endings. All of them don't. Each one, regardless of how it ends, further convinces me that "I'm Number One" living leads only to frustration and despair. We should continually praise God for delivering us from that despair.

FOR REFLECTION

1. What human attitude does the title of this chapter describe?

2. What does putting others ahead of yourself do for you personally?

3. What was the main difference between the 0-10 team and the 9-1 team as described in this chapter?

4. How does this same attitude affect other relationships that surround you each day?

5. What can you do to have "winning teams" wherever you go? (We're not talking about scoreboard victory here.)

12

What about the Loser?

"You're today's winner on 'The Price is Right'!"

"You've won the Big Deal of the day!"

"Thank you, Brent, and here we are in the locker room of the new Super Bowl champions. It is so noisy and exciting down here I can hardly hear myself talk!"

"I finally broke it off with her. I feel so much better now."

But how does *she* feel? Everyone loves to talk about winners, but how does the *loser* feel? What about the loser?

I know how she feels. I know how the losing team feels. The loser is hurting. I've been there too many times.

Have you ever noticed on TV game shows and sports events how well-trained the cameramen are? They only show the winners' faces. No one wants to see the sadness and disappointment on the faces of the losers! Of course, when you enter the football arena you know you'll either win or lose. That's the name of the game, and at least you are prepared for the possibility of losing. When you make an appearance on "The Price Is Right," you know your chances of winning the showcase are about one in twelve. But in relationships it is different. There doesn't have to be a loser. But often there is, and there is real hurt. And that hurt doesn't go away, out of our line of vision as it does on TV game shows.

Yesterday a very outgoing, happy (I thought), attractive fifteen-year-old girl called me. When I asked her how she was doing, she said, "Great." I sensed this wasn't true. When I asked her how she was *really* doing, she said she was hurting. "What's wrong, Sara?" I asked. "I tried to kill myself," was her quiet reply.

"Why?"

"My friends. They kept hurting me." As the conversation went on she told me how she was still hurting inside but was so glad she didn't die. Like all the others I've talked to who lived through their attempt to take their lives, she was so happy she was still alive.

If someone is your friend, you don't hurt them. If you call a girl your girlfriend or tell her you love her, you don't pull the rug out from under her. You don't abandon her in her time of need. Almost a million teenage girls go through the abortion clinics each year. (And believe me, none of them like it. All of them hurt deeply because of it.) Almost all of the "losers" (the babies whose lives are ended) die alone. Where are the fathers? The mothers are almost always alone. Where are their lovers? Lovers? They "made love," but where are they now?

A sixteen-year-old guy ran past me in the airport in Denver. His T-shirt bore the now familiar phrase "Happiness is scoring" (a street line for getting a girl into bed). If it is so happy, then why does the girl hurt so badly when the boy leaves her?

AC/DC, Kiss, Prince, David Bowie and all the rest prance across the stage with millions of dollars flowing into their pockets and millions of cheers from mesmerized fans filling their egos. They sing about the happiness of drugs, sex with anyone, the easy solution of suicide, and the party in hell.

What about the loser? What about the lonely mom whose son listens to their lies and takes his life? What about the millions of drug addicts and hopeless alcoholics who followed the destructive path of their egotistical heroes?

Millions of teenage girls idolize Brooke Shields and her beautiful, sensuous TV face. Little girls idolize their Brooke Shields dolls, the teenagers admire her body as she undresses in front of the camera to entice her latest lover. She's so successful. She's a real winner by worldly standards. But what about the girl who tries in real life to follow the beauty-success route, only to feel the hurt of "two hundred knives going through her" when her "boyfriend" left her after he got what he wanted? It's easy to keep our minds focused on Brooke—or Madonna—or whoever is popular at the moment. It's easy to forget about the real people we know, people who are often deeply hurt when their lives don't match those of the media figures they idolize.

Boys, "I'm Third" means respecting the girl's needs more than you love your needs. "I'm Third" means protecting her purity more than you protect your desires for conquest. Hear me, girls: "I'm Third" means dressing modestly, kissing modestly, holding hands modestly, talking modestly so as not to arouse your boyfriend to begin his mind in the dangerous process. "I'm Third" means caring for the would-be loser! Today and every day all of us need to run an image across our minds of our boyfriend or girlfriend, our friends, and our parents. Are we making them feel like winners, or are we making losers out of them?

I'll never forget the sting I felt when I walked into the bedroom of my house and my first wife of fourteen months looked at me and said, "I don't love you anymore. I love your best friend." Soon she was gone. I was a loser. It hurts me to this day. (I really never blamed her and don't even now. I know I could have been a better husband and more sensitive to her needs. But being a loser hurts.)

Let's make winners out of our dates. Let's make winners out of our parents. Let's make winners out of our friends. Build them up. Listen to their hurts, and begin the healing process. Treat them like Jesus himself would treat them if he were in your place.

FOR REFLECTION

1. Why is so much attention focused on the beautiful, sexy, talented winner and so little concern given to the loser who is the victim of the "winner's" fake life-style as portrayed on TV?

2. How does it feel to be a loser?

3. How can you make winners out of the people who are close to you?

4. What can you do on a larger scale to change the trend in America and the world that is producing so many "losers" in young, vulnerable guys and girls?

13
I'm Third

*I*magine a crazy scene with me for a moment. You have just dozed off after an exhausting night of study. You are awakened by the rumble of a finely tuned engine, followed by the persistent honking of a horn. You peek out of your bedroom window and see me in your driveway, standing by the most beautiful car you have ever seen! I'm waving my arms wildly and a smile is beaming from my face as I call your name and tell you to come outside in a hurry! As you grab your clothes and run outside your eyes fairly "pop out" when you behold a brand new Maseratti. Your fingertips run smoothly across the bright red, hand-lacquered finish. I look you in the eye and say, "It's yours."

"What did you say?"

"I said, 'It's yours.'"

"You're crazy!" You are laughing and shouting as you jump into the car of your dreams! To your further amazement, as you get into this four wheels of mysterious fascination you see my briefcase propped open on the passenger seat, revealing its contents: stacks of one-hundred-dollar bills. You fairly faint as you look up and say, "Uh, is this mine, too?"

"Yes," I reply, "all yours. A million dollars."

"What's the catch?" you ask. "What did I do to deserve this?"

"Nothing."

"Nothing?"

"No, not really. You see, you're my friend and I love you and I want to give you—" Before I finish you jump out of the car screaming with excitement! You throw your arms around my neck and squeeze me so tight I think my head will fall off!

"Oh, thank you, thank you, thank you!"

"Could I ask you a favor?"

"Sure, ask me anything."

"Would you meet me for breakfast tomorrow at 7:00 A.M. just so we can talk for awhile?"

"Yeah, sure. Simple, man!"

"One other thing," I pursue. "Don't dent up the car. If you drive it too fast or down a low, bumpy road or drive too close to undergrowth on the side of a road, it will begin to rip apart. Keep it washed and waxed regularly. OK?"

"Sure, yeah, sure. What else?"

"That's about all, just take care of the car and spend the money wisely. By the way, do you love me?"

"Sure! Absolutely! I loooovvve you!" As you jump into your new dream car and streak down the driveway I hear your screaming assurance of love.

It wouldn't be too hard to meet my simple requests

if I loved you that much, would it? You want to know something surprising? In less than ten years the Maseratti would be practically worn out and the briefcase would be empty. No question you would have enjoyed the moments of exhilaration given you, but the day would come when the party would be over.

What if I could promise you a happy forever? I mean (as my little kids say when they want to know if you're talking make-believe or FOR REAL) in REAL life! Yes, in Real Life, God promises a crown of victory, a personal mansion in heaven, and a fulfilling, purposeful time on this planet to all of his adopted sons and daughters, sincere believers in Jesus Christ.

Would you believe God loves you? Would you do the things he asks you to do to keep your precious body and your mind from harm? Would you tell him you love him by gladly meeting his demands designed to protect you and provide for your future?

I can't begin to describe to you how much I love my four precious children. I think about them almost constantly. To pick up my little baby boy and kiss his chubby little cheek as he squirms and giggles in my arms is more fulfilling than anything in the world. When I am traveling I am almost always homesick. To please my little "buddies" gives me the deepest satisfaction.

One day as I carried my flaxen-haired youngest girl to the car, I gave her a squeeze and said (for the umpteenth time!), "Courtney, I really do love you!"

"Do you love me as much as Jesus does?" was Courtney's typically candid and outspoken reply.

"What?" I stalled for time as I gulped.

"Daddy, do you love me as much as Jesus does?"

"No, baby, I don't," I stuttered.

"Why not?"

"Well, doll, I just don't. . . . I mean, I love you with all my heart, but Jesus . . . his heart is so much bigger than mine is!"

I'll never forget that day. I'll never forget what I said because it's so true! As much as I love my foursome, I don't ever come close to giving the quantity or quality of love that God has for one of his children. He loves you so completely, so wisely, so tenderly!

Over and over in Scripture God assures us of his love—a billion times greater than any car ever fashioned in a European assembly line! With the promises come his love-filled commandments to strive diligently to worship him regularly and bring every area of your life under the control of his wise and caring hand.

"And I will be a father to you, and you shall be sons and daughters to Me," says the Lord Almighty. Therefore, having these promises, beloved, let us cleanse ourselves from all defilement of flesh and spirit, perfecting holiness in the fear of God (2 Corinthians 6:18–7:1).

"Perfecting holiness," Paul says. You'll be happy to compare that demand to a daily trip through the car wash for the imaginary Maseratti—plus a hand-rubbed wax job, regular oil changes, only the finest fuel, and selected smooth roads to travel, etc. You could provide a daily "car wash" for yourself by confessing your mistakes sincerely. The hand-rubbed polish could be applied as you agree with God to turn wholeheartedly from those mistakes and follow him in each area of your life. God's will for you is that you think and act like Jesus did. As an eighty-two-year-old friend of mine told me as he expressed God's love through the kindest eyes I've ever known, "You see, Joe, God was so in love with his Son that he wanted a whole lot more of us to be just like him."

When you have your first baby, your "little bundle of joy" (and these words are usually quite true) will go through the "terrible twos" or "threes." Most babies go through stages of testing their parents' authority. (Yes, I went through mine and you probably did, too!)

Isn't it amazing how often you find people in their terrible twos at age sixteen, twenty, thirty, fifty,—testing God and trying their heavenly Parent's authority instead of lovingly submitting to it? Paul, in 1 Corinthians 13:11, spells out the need for growth: "When I was a child, I used to speak as a child, think as a child, reason as a child; when I became a man, I did away with childish things."

God has blessed Debbie Jo and me with four children—four little chubby packages who laughed and hugged and kissed us through their early years. They had their moments, but for the most part they were (and are) so eager to please, so excited about doing things together with an appreciative mom and daddy! Do you think my foursome get the best their daddy can give them? Or do you think I have to beat them into submission? Let me tell you, I'd do anything for those precious children of mine—anything that's good for them, that is.

Your relationship with Christ was never meant to be that of a fearful slave and tyrannical master! It's to be like a loving father with a loving child. And God wants his children to be the best. They can be the best when they are committed to a Father that they love and trust completely. In that trust there is fulfillment.

My walk with Christ is indescribably fulfilling. Are there tears? Sure! Sometimes the tears are the result of joy I can't contain when I remember my wife in the magic of childbirth or catch my mind wandering in the paradise of my fourteen-year-old love of my little wife. Sometimes the tears are those of sorrow when a loved one dies or when I hold a hurt child. To be very honest with you, many of my tears come when I just think quietly about how much God has forgiven me. How could he love me enough to die for me? It is too overwhelming to fathom sometimes!

As I try to fathom the deep love of God, I am more and more aware of the need for *holiness*. God is holy and pure, and he wants us to be that way. In the Psalms, David wrote, "I will set no worthless thing before my eyes" (Psalm 101:3). David didn't want anything to hinder his clear vision of God. When you are that committed to staying that close to God, you will enjoy a love for holiness and purity, things precious to God.

I'm excited about pursuing purity because God wants me to be pure. He commands me to be Christlike.

God also wants *me* to love me. He knows I can't when I feel guilty and unforgiven. He knows I don't like myself when I think about my past mistakes, and he knows that the only power I have over the past is purity in the present.

As one girl wrote to me, "When I live like God wants me to live, I feel good about me!"

With God's unconditional love to launch you into the flight of purity over all the sin that surrounds you, you can be committed to Christ-like living!

An inquisitive eight-year-old girl poked her head under the newspaper of her father who was busy reading about the day's events. She looked up into his face and said, "Daddy, can we live our lives pure like God wants us to?"

"No way. You know that's impossible. No one is perfect." He attempted to brush her off with his brisk reply.

The dad went back to his sports page, but the little girl persisted. "Dad, do you think we can live like Jesus did for a whole year?"

"No, you know that's impossible!" he snapped.

"Dad, can we live pure for a month?"

"No, absolutely not!" He was getting disturbed.

"A week?"

"No."

"A day?"

"No!"

"Dad, can we live like God wants us to for a minute? Just a minute?"

"I suppose," the dad hurriedly concluded. "I suppose we could live purely for a minute."

"Then, Dad, why don't we live our lives a minute at a time?"

As you try to live the pure life, you know you will make mistakes. But remember, every mistake you ever made (or will make) is paid for. God loves you that much. In his eyes you are a perfect "10" the moment you confess and turn from your sins and receive him into your heart as Lord and Savior. With that blessed assurance you can live your life "a minute at a time"—in purity and in honor of God's love for you.

When I try,
I fail.
When I trust in him,
he succeeds!

FOR REFLECTION

1. *When God says, "I will be a father to you," what is he saying about his love toward you personally?*

2. *Why is it important for you to understand that love?*

3. *When you see yourself as God sees you, what does that do to your self-image?*

4. *Why is it important to love yourself?*

5. *What is he asking you to do when he asks you to "cleanse yourself from all defilement of flesh and spirit, perfecting holiness" in your life?*

6. *Why does God want you to be Christ-like?*

7. *Name some specific areas that you need to change today to be more Christ-like.*

8. *How can you begin to live your life "a minute at a time" today?*

14

The Man Who Matched Our Mountains*

*O*ut of the sun, packed in a diamond and flying as one, the Minute Men dove at nearly the speed of sound toward a tiny emerald patch on Ohio's unwrinkled crazy quilt below.

It was a little after nine in the morning and the target the Air National Guard's jet precision team was diving at was famed Wright-Patterson Air Force Base, just outside Dayton, Ohio.

On the ground several thousand faces looked upward as Colonel Ward Williams, leader of the Denver-based Sabrejet team, gauged the high-speed pullout.

For the young West Point cadets and for the multitude of civilians who watched, the corps de ballet perfection of the red Sabre acro-team was a thing of awe and wonder. For the Minute Men pilots, Walt Williams,

---

*This chapter is about an "I'm Third" man who gave his life to save the lives of many others. He and his sons grew up in Kanakuk Kamps, where I had also spent my summers. This story, written by Ed Mack Miller, is from *The Denver Post*, December 3, 1961, and is reprinted by permission.

Captain Bob Cherry, Lieutenant Bob Odle, Captain John Ferrier, and Major Win Coomer, it was routine. They had given their show hundreds of times before several million people from Spokane, Washington, to Jacksonville, Florida, and from Burlington, Vermont, to Honolulu, showing the people of the United States how proficient a reserve unit can be, telling with speed and thrills and swift smoke-strokes across the sky the Air National Guard story. For the Minute Men this was just another show, but they were glad the crowd was good, the skies were clear, and the air was morning-smooth.

Low across the fresh green grass the jet team streaked, far ahead of the planes' own noise. Judging the pull up, Colonel Williams pressed the microphone button on top his throttle: "Smoke on—now."

Then the diamond of planes was pulling straight up into the turquoise sky, a bushy tail of white smoke pluming out behind the formation.

The crowd gasped when the four ships suddenly separated, rolling to the four points of the compass and leaving a beautiful, smoky fleur-de-lis inscribed on the background blue of the sky.

This was the Minute Men's famed "flower burst" maneuver. For a minute the crowd relaxed, gazing at the tranquil beauty of the huge white flower that had grown from the verdant Ohio grasslands to fill the great bowl of sky.

Out on the end of his arm of the flower, Colonel Williams turned his Sabre hard, cut off the smoke trail, and dropped the nose of his F-86 to pick up speed for the low-altitude cross-over maneuver. Then glancing back over his shoulder, he froze.

Far across the sky to the east, John Ferrier's plane was rolling. He was in trouble. And his plane was headed right for the small town of Fairborn, on the edge of Patterson field. In a moment the lovely morning turned to horror. Everyone saw, everyone understood. One of the planes was out of control.

Racing his Sabre in the direction of the crippled plane, Colonel Williams raised his voice over the mike. "Bail out, Johnny, bail out!" There was still plenty of time, still plenty of room. Twice more Williams issued the command. Each time he was answered by a blip of smoke. He grasped the sense of it immediately. John Ferrier couldn't reach the mike button on the throttle because he had both hands tugging on a control stick that was locked full-throw right. But the smoke button was on the stick, and he was answering the only way he could—squeezing it to tell Walt he thought he could pull out . . . that he couldn't let his airplane go into the houses of Fairborn.

Captain John T. Ferrier's Sabrejet hit the ground equidistant from four houses. There was hardly any place other than that one backyard garden where he could have hit without killing people.

There was a tremendous explosion which knocked a woman and several children to the ground. But no one was hurt—with the exception of Captain Ferrier. He was killed instantly.

Major Win Coomer, who had flown with Ferrier for years, both in the Air National Guard and on United Airlines, and had served a combat tour with him in Korea, was the first Minute Man to land at Patterson

AFB after the crash. He got a car and raced to the crash scene.

He found a neighborhood still stunned from the awful thing that had happened. But there was no resentment as is ordinarily the case when a peaceful community is torn by a crash. A steady stream of people came to tall, handsome graying Win Coomer who stood—still in his flying suit—beside the smoking, gaping hole in the ground where his best friend had died. And, humbly, they all said the same thing: This man died for us.

"A bunch of us were standing together, watching the show," an elderly man told Coomer, "when he started to roll. He was headed straight for us. For a second I felt that we looked right at each other." There were tears in the man's eyes. "Then he pulled up right over us and put it in there."

Ferrier's teammates figured he used the plane's rudders to steer the crippled plane away from the people and houses.

It was a bold and courageous last act. But it was not an act alien to the nature of John T. Ferrier, who had been awarded one of the nation's most outstanding medals of courage and bravery for risking his life "beyond the call of duty" in Korea to fly cover over a downed Marine pilot until helicopter rescue could come. On that sortie the pilot's own fellow fliers had been afraid to fly down into the hell of flak and ground fire to keep the Communist ground troops from the downed airman. Ferrier and a fellow Air Force flier had taken their F-51s down voluntarily and "capped" the pilot until help had come, even though

Ferrier had limped home with a rocket hole "as big as Korea" in his wing.

Denverites remembered Johnny Ferrier as an outstanding Colorado University tailback in football, as an All-City softball player, and an A.A.U. Champion handball player and a wonderful family man who neither drank nor smoked (his worst expletives were "dad-gum it" or "dad-burn it").

The number of cars in his funeral procession was the largest in the memory of the people who attended. Traffic was halted for miles. Many people came who had never known John Ferrier, but they had heard the story of his courageous death, and they came out of respect to the memory of a man who died a real hero.

In a letter to John Ferrier's widow, Governor Steve McNichols of Colorado wrote: "I know that you and your children can always be proud as we are of the fact that in his last moments he used his skill and his concern for humanity in protecting others from the terrible mishap."

There were other letters of comfort for Tulie Ferrier and the three Ferrier children. Brigadier General Donald L. Hardy, commander of Wright-Patterson, said, "Eyewitness reports indicate that the plane was headed directly for people and houses in the area, and that a definite attempt was made by your husband to miss these. May you find comfort in the fact that his attempt was successful."

A Dayton housewife wrote: "This was a brave man who preferred to guide his plane into an open space away from his fellow man rather than save himself and chance the death of others."

U.S. Senator Gordon Allott said: "His skill, both as a member of the Minute Men and as a United Airlines pilot has been a credit to himself and his family. His shining heroism in the split second over Ohio will serve as a constant example to all of us."

It was Senator Allott who called long-distance from Washington on September 26, 1957, to inform Tulie Ferrier that the United States government had recognized John Ferrier's final act of courage by awarding him, posthumously, the Distinguished Flying Cross. . . .

As one Air Guard officer commented, "An American poet, Sam Foss, once wrote, 'Bring me men to match my mountains.' Well, Ferrier was one of those men. . . .

"We don't have to fear any enemy as long as America can produce people of the stature of John Ferrier."

[The article from *The Denver Post* concludes here. The remainder of this chapter is by Joe White.]

●　　　●　　　●

Shortly after the crash, Johnny's wife wrote Kanakuk Kamps (where I live and work) the following letter in which she referred to the "I'm Third" card (like the one that was slipped into this book) that Johnny had received at camp many years before. The man in charge of the camp at that time was named Coach Bill Lantz. He talked "I'm Third" often and lived "I'm Third" every day.

Here's a copy of Tulie Ferrier's letter:

Coach, I went through his billfold last night and found the old worn card which he always carried—"I'm Third." He told me once he got it from you; you had stressed it at one of your camp sermons. Anyway, he may have had a few faults—but they were few and minor, but he followed that creed to the "T" and certainly to the very end. God is first, the other fellow second, and "I'm Third"—not just the day he died but long before that—certainly as long as I've known him. I'm going to carry that same card with me from now on and see if it won't serve me as a reminder. I shouldn't need it, but I'm sure I do as I have many more faults than he.

God First
  Others Second
    And I'm Third

The happy way to live. The loving way to live. The only way to really live.

FOR REFLECTION

1. *Why didn't Johnny Ferrier bail out?*

2. *What had he been doing his whole life to get ready for that one historic decision?*

3. *What does putting "God first" mean to you now?*

4. *What does it mean to you to put the "other person second"?*

5. *What does it mean to you to be "I'm Third"?*

6. *What changes do you see taking place in your life as you understand what it means to be "I'm Third"?*